Query Letters That Worked!

Real queries that landed $2K+ writing assignments

D0911089

Query Letters That Worked!

Real queries that landed $2K+ writing assignments

Angela Hoy

Publisher, WritersWeekly.com

With Gratitude

I'd like to personally thank each of the highly successful writers appearing in *Query Letters That Worked!* Only through the guidance of our most successful peers will we learn how to succeed in this industry. Even though I offered cash for the opportunity to publish real query letters that landed high-paying assignments, not everyone invited to contribute to this book was willing to share their secrets with the rest of us. The ones who did, whose queries appear herein, deserve a big hug! Thanks guys and gals!

I'd also like to thank Autumn Manka, the managing editor at WritersWeekly.com, for helping me organize my notes. What a mess!

A huge thanks to Julie Sartain for her beautiful cover art. She's a multi-talented lady! You can see samples of her work at: http://www.JulesAvenueGraphics.com

As always, my eternal gratitude goes out to my friend, M.J. Rose, for her sound advice, loving support, and eternal enthusiasm. M.J. is an incredible author and teaches outstanding and fun classes for other authors! See: http://www.mjrose.com

And, once again, warm fuzzies and love to my hubby, Richard, and my children, Zach, Ali, Frank, and Max, for patiently enduring many nights of take-out dinners and a backlog of laundry while I researched, organized, wrote, re-wrote, edited, and re-edited this book again, and again, and again, and...

Table of Contents

Introduction

Every day at WritersWeekly.com, we receive emails from writers requesting advice on how to write better query letters. While we're always happy to give free advice, there's a much better way to learn - by studying and emulating real, successful query letters!

In these pages, you'll find copies of real query letters that landed lucrative writing assignments for their authors worth $2,000 or more. Above each query, you'll read about and receive advice from the authors of these queries. And, while you can't copy these query letters word-for-word (they're copyrighted) and submit them to publications, you can emulate their style and use the advice contained herein to improve your own query letters.

After the section on query letters and proposals, you'll find a section featuring real pitch letters that resulted in writing assignments worth $2,000 or more. Rather than querying a specific article idea, each "pitch" letter was submitted by the writer in an attempt to secure future, ongoing assignments from that publication (be added to their stable of freelancers!). If you're looking for steady freelance writing work (like all of us!), don't miss the general pitch letters section!

At WritersWeekly.com, we publish more than 100 articles each year. Since 1997, I have, personally, read and evaluated all queries received by WritersWeekly.com and reviewed thousands of book proposals submitted to our publishing company, Booklocker.com. Above each query and pitch letter appearing in this book, I have added my opinion on what items in each make it a "hit."

Since editors often jump around from publication to publication, we have removed their names from the queries. And, since publications move as well, we have removed addresses and other contact information. If you wish to contact a publication featured in this book, please find their current contact information at their website. We have included information on how each editor was addressed in each query letter (i.e. first name only, full name, etc.).

We reformatted the queries to fit this book's page format but, other than that, they appear as they did during submission. You may even find the occasional typo or grammatical error in a query! Sometimes, query letters are so enticing that editors overlook the errors. Any errors appearing in the queries here were ignored or not noticed by the publication's editors.

As with any book that offers hints from numerous professionals, you're going to read conflicting advice. However, each method mentioned works for each writer.

I encourage you to click on each author's website, where provided, to see how they present their professional writing businesses to editors online. You'll find examples of résumés, writing samples, online clips, and more to help you create and/or improve your own website, resume, and presentation of clips. And, you are welcome to contact the writers with questions through the contact information provided on their websites. They'll be very happy to hear from you!

Query Letters and Proposals

Woman's Day - $2,100

Judy Gruen is the author of Till We Eat Again: Confessions of a Diet Dropout (Champion Press, 2003) and Carpool Tunnel Syndrome: Motherhood as Shuttle Diplomacy (Champion Press, 2002). She also writes the popular "Off My Noodle" humor column, available by subscribing at http://www.judygruen.com. Her columns frequently appear on SanityCentral.com, Homebodies.org, and other sites. Before writing books, Judy wrote features and essays on a variety of topics, including health care subjects. She also worked as an editor for Accepted.com, an editorial advisory service for prospective graduate students. Judy has written essays and features for Ladies' Home Journal, Woman's Day, First for Women and Family Circle. She attributes her success in finally breaking into the major magazines to having published her books. Read more about Judy at: http://www.judygruen.com

~~~~~

Judy Gruen has worked on many projects that brought in more than $2,000, but the only one resulting from an actual query letter was a story she wrote for *Woman's Day* about the importance of family rituals.

Judy used a topic she found in a recognized professional trade journal, and put a family spin on it. Not only was the topic unique and interesting, but she also pitched interviews with medical professionals, which added validity to her query claims.

After backing up her editorial with data from a medical publication, Judy tied the topic to all families, making it of obvious interest to readers of *Woman's Day*. Judy then explains exactly what she will provide in the article, including a list of specific examples.

She offers a sidebar (this is not only attractive to readers, but also increases the word count, which means higher pay in most cases). And, Judy provides a list of possibilities on getting celebrities involved in the article. Agents are often happy to obtain statements from their celebrity clients for large magazines such as *Woman's Day*. And, readers love to read about celebrities' personal lives.

What makes Judy's query a hit:
1. Uses information from a professional journal to prove legitimacy of idea.
2. Ties professional article to topic appealing to all families.
3. Offers interviews with medical professionals.
4. Offers sidebar.
5. Offers celebrity tie-in.

The query was sent on Judy's personal letterhead by mail. While Judy already had a relationship with this editor, she was still required to pitch her story idea using a query letter.

Judy's $2,100 Query

Judy Gruen
Street Address
City, State, Zip
Phone Number
Email Address

Date

Editor's Full Name
Associate Health Editor
Woman's Day
Mailing Address
City, State, Zip

Dear [Editor's First Name],

It's no secret that rituals help bond families together, but is there more to the Sunday morning pancake breakfast than just fun and food? In fact, a report in the current issue of the Journal of Family Psychology concluded that family rituals do enhance emotional and even physical health. Lead researcher Barbara Fiese, a psychologist at Syracuse University in New York, notes that even something as subtle as greeting people when they come into the house at the end of the day, adds to the creation of a harmonious and stable family life.

The study analyzed 32 previous studies and included investigations of families with young children, with adolescents and with a single parent. Kids who participated in regular family rituals, even eating dinner as a family several times a week, performed better in school and were calmer than those who lacked such rituals.

While the study may simply confirm what many of us feel is common sense, the scientific "proof" is an excellent reminder of how important these rituals can be. In a "Favorite Family Rituals" story for Woman's Day, I would include five or ten such family rituals that add to that indelible feeling of closeness. Here are a few possibilities:

- At dinner, asking kids about the best part of their day, the worst part of their day, and their hopes for tomorrow
- Watching movies together and eating popcorn on Saturday night
- Hiking or other outdoor activities on weekends
- Attending church or synagogue together each week
- Volunteering with a civic or church-sponsored organization. (One family I know helps pack and deliver food once a week to needy residents in town.)

As a bonus, I think your readers would enjoy a sidebar in which celebrities and child-rearing experts share their own favorite family rituals. These might include:

Actress and author Patricia Heaton
(*Motherhood and Hollywood: How to Get a Job Like Mine*)

Journalist and author Maria Shriver
(*Ten Things I Wish I'd Known Before I Went Out Into the Real World*)

Motivational speaker Zig Ziglar
(*Raising Positive Kids in a Negative World*)

Dr. James Dobson, author of numerous books on the family, most recently of the bestseller *Bringing Up Boys*

The Today Show's Al Roker
(*Don't Make Me Stop This Car! Adventures in Fatherhood*)

Marie Osmond
(*Behind the Smile: My Journey out of Post-Partum Depression*)

Demi Moore (who moved her family to Idaho to give them a more "normal" childhood)

Actress and comedienne Carol Burnett.

[Editor's First Name], as always, I look forward to working with you and providing quality content for Woman's Day.

Best Wishes,
Judy Gruen

Ladies' Home Journal - $3,000

Judy Gruen's bio can be found in the preceding chapter.

~~~~~

In her *Ladies' Home Journal* query below, Judy Gruen begins by reminding the editor of their recent conversation (so the editor will remember this is not a cold query). She then states why she believes the ideas will be successful (sometimes editors need a little help seeing how an article may interest their readership). Note: She says she "believes", not that she "knows." Some editors get upset when writers give the impression they know the magazine's readers better than the editor.

Later in the query, Judy offers to work with the editor to adapt the ideas to their needs. This shows flexibility and friendliness. You can almost see Judy smiling right there on paper. She also subtly mentions that she'd like to provide more ideas in the future. The editor will then not be surprised when Judy sends more ideas to her in the future, and addresses her directly regarding their past correspondence.

What makes Judy's query a hit:
1. Reminds editor of recent conversation.
2. Mentions why article may be of interest to her readers.
3. Is not pushy (says "believes"; not "knows").
4. Offers to adapt the idea to editor's specific needs.
5. Very friendly!

We have only included Judy's successful query letter below (there were three in her batch). *Ladies' Home Journal* paid Judy $3,000 for her article. The interesting twist in this job is that the magazine was completely revamped during that timeframe and the article has not yet been published. But, Judy was still paid for her work!

Judy's $3,000 Query

Judy Gruen
Street Address
City, State, Zip
Phone Number
Email Address

Date

Editor's Full Name
Articles Editor
Ladies' Home Journal
Mailing Address
City, State, Zip

Dear Ms. [Editor's Last Name],

Thanks so much for taking the time to speak with me yesterday about my story ideas for Ladies' Home Journal's "That's Life" column. As we discussed, I have worked up proposals for the three topics you liked: "Nutritional Nabobs," "Tradition, Tradition," and "Who's That Person in Enormous Shoes Who's Calling Me Mommy?"

I believe all three ideas have great potential for both humor and insight, and over time I hope to offer you more fresh ideas as well. I'm open to discussing any adaptations or changes to these proposals so that the finished essays will best serve your readership. I appreciate your consideration of my work and look forward to speaking with you again soon.

Sincerely,
Judy Gruen

"Who's That Person in Enormous Shoes Who's Calling Me Mommy?"

I'm now buying my oldest son, aged 12, shoes in the men's department. In a pinch, he and his dad can swap shoes if necessary. Unlike my husband, however, my eldest son has also taken to spending inordinate amounts of time gelling his hair, trying to get the little flip in the front just so. The other day I spotted some dark downy hair on his upper lip. Very soon, perhaps even next Tuesday, I'll have to look up to yell at him. But despite all that, instead of always calling "Mom!" when he wants me he slips up occasionally and still calls me Mommy. It won't last long, but it's music to my ears.

In an essay about mothering this growing son, my eldest of three sons and one daughter, I'd talk about trying to respect his budding independence while keeping a finger on the pulse of his life, trying to balance his increasing need for privacy with my need to keep our lines of communication flowing: "Hey, how about those Lakers?" I might jovially ask this sports addict, only to hear, "You're a little out of date, Mom. They got ripped last night by the Bulls." Oh well, can't say I'm not trying.

It's a scary time to be a parent, especially of teens, and I'm not even talking about the food bills. How do I keep him tethered to my love and values, yet give him enough freedom to make mistakes that are necessary for maturity? How long will I still be his favorite woman, or be replaced by a girl named Dakota who wears low-slung jeans advertising her bellybutton? I've got to put myself into his shoes, at least figuratively, so I can see things through his eyes. There are lots of opportunities to strengthen the connection. Sometimes we play a game of gin rummy after homework is done. Sometimes I just ask, "What's going on?" to let him know I'm here in spirit as well as body. It's a tall order for a short mom, but I'm working on it day by day.

Family Fun Magazine - $2,000

Sharon Miller Cindrich is a freelance writer whose work has appeared in magazines and newspapers nationwide, including Family Fun Magazine, The Writer, and The Chicago Tribune. She is currently working on a feature article for Parenting Magazine.

~~~~~

Sharon Miller Cindrich had previously pitched several ideas to this publication without luck. But, her professionalism and creativity were so impressive that the editors asked her to pitch an article on this topic (it was their general idea, but Sharon came up with the craft ideas). Even in the query letter, Sharon's warmth and love for her children are apparent, and editors will assume this warmth will also be portrayed in her final article.

Sharon summarizes the article by offering to send samples of the actual crafts for the editor to enjoy. And, Sharon delivered the crafts with the final article so the magazine's photographers could include beautiful, glossy photos for readers.

What makes Sharon's query a hit:
1. Offers professionalism and detail despite the fact that it was the editor's article idea.
2. Warmth and love are obvious in her query (for an article that targets families).
3. Humor and creativity are inspiring and enthusiasm is infectious. Makes you want to go to her house, sit down at her table, and help with the fun!

This query was sent via email. *Family Fun Magazine* paid Sharon $2,000 for her article.

Note: Don't miss the Snowman Scraps paragraph below. Hilarious!

Sharon's $2,000 Query

Since the holiday season can leave us all running around for last minute presents, pageants and parties, this year my children and I devised a way to spread some holiday cheer, trim the tree, and celebrate the season's festivities with a couple of close friends in what we're calling our Holiday Ornament Workshop.

Visions of sugar plums aren't the only thing dancing around in the heads of my six- and eight-year-old, who love rolling up their sleeves, covering the dining room table with a plastic cloth and piling it with art supplies. To keep things fun, but low key, we pair up with just one other family and when our guests arrive, glitter and glue and glad tidings fill the air. We play holiday music, eat, drink and create merriment with hand-fashioned baubles and trinkets, knick-knacks and doo-dads that are as delightful to make as they are to hang on the tree.

Homemade ornaments have always been a tradition at our home. They are the perfect personal gift for family and friends, a great way to create a holiday keepsake each year, and wonderful outlet for children who are filled with anticipation and excited energy weeks before the celebrations begin.

Here are just a few ideas I have for extraordinary ornaments using simple, ordinary supplies:

Snowman Garland: Turn a traditional popcorn garland into a snowman theme by alternating popcorn with mini-marshmallows (for snowballs). String a large marshmallow every six inches and create smiling snowman faces on those using fine point magic markers. Dab with craft glue and sprinkle with glitter to create snowy strings of winter wonder.

Giving Hands: These easy paper ornaments are a fun and adorable way to reinforce the importance of giving during the holidays. Fold a piece of colored paper in half and trace your child's hand so that the pinkie falls on the fold. Cut out the paper hand, keeping the fold in tact. You will now have a pair of hands that can open and close in a card fashion. Have your children decorate the outside and tape a special surprise (a coin, a piece of candy or a special message) inside the palm of one of the hands. Close the hands, punch a hole through the wrist section and tie with a colorful bow for hanging. For an even easier rendition, trace your child's hand mitten style and decorate accordingly.

Tinfoil Icicle: This effect is so easy, it's almost not worth instructions. Mold tinfoil into an icicle shape. Use either a traditional hanger or a piece of black thread for hanging. Create a bunch in a variety of sizes for a great effect on your holiday tree, a window or a long staircase. This ornament is perfect for even the smallest hands and ideal for outdoor decorating.

Cookie Cutter Cuties: Real cookies may be too fragile (and tempting) for your tree, however, you can create look alike cookies cut from brown paper bags that look almost good enough to eat. Use your favorite cookie cutters to trace cookie shapes on brown paper bags. Then, spread on the icing (white paint mixed with glue) and sprinkle with, what else, your favorite real sprinkles.

Paint Balls: Though this may sound messy, these ornaments give a big effect with very little mess. Fill a clear glass ball ornament (available at your craft store) with 1/3 red paint and 1/3 green paint (or any colors you like.) Then gently turn the ball so that the colors cover the inside, creating a magnificent pattern. Do not pour excess paint out, as it will change your pattern. While there is very little mess, these ornaments take several days to dry completely, so put them in a safe place for at least 4 or 5 days before hanging.

Santa Hat Cones: Put a Saint Nick spin on these hanging treat cups, by creating cones out of red construction paper. Staple a white ribbon across the top for hanging. For the white fur trim, pull apart cotton balls and glue around the top opening of the cone. Add one last cotton ball at the pointed end, and sprinkle lightly with fine glitter. Kids can hang these on the tree and see what Santa fills them with, or fill with treats yourself and let holiday guests take one when they stop by.

Of course, all this creating is sure to make crafters hungry. I keep energy levels up by supplying kids with bowls of **Snowman Scraps**: a grab and munch mixture of marshmallows (snowballs), candy corn (noses), raisins (buttons, eyes) and small pretzel sticks (arms).

Deanna, I hope this gives you an idea of how I would approach this story. I've tried to keep a balance of holiday designs that apply and appeal to a variety of winter celebrations. Let me know if you have a difficult time visualizing any of these ornaments, they are much cuter in real life than in the writing. I'm looking forward to your feedback! (And to Christmas, writing this has really put me in the holiday spirit!)

Cheers,

Sharon

Family Fun Magazine - $2,000

Sharon Miller Cindrich's bio appears in the preceding chapter.

~~~~~

As soon as the former story (see previous chapter) was wrapped up, Sharon quickly took advantage of her fresh rapport with the editor to pitch another story. She says, "I had the editor's attention and they knew I could deliver."

Sharon begins by reminding the editor of her recent assignment while complimenting the editor she worked with. Her tone is professional, but also very pleasant. Her article idea is outstanding and she summarizes by suggesting the perfect issue for the article.

What makes Sharon's query a hit:
1. Immediately follows a successful, timely, and quality article delivery.
2. Reminds editor of existing relationship (it's often difficult for busy editors to remember every writer's name or recent article).
3. Professional yet friendly.
4. Unique idea and suggests the perfect issue for publication.

What follows is Sharon's quick query, sent via email. *Family Fun Magazine* paid Sharon $3,400 for her article.

Sharon's $3,400 Query

[Editor's First Name],

Just a note to say thanks for the opportunity on the Ornament Workshop. The ornaments and story have been handed in and I am just waiting to hear back. [Other Editor's First Name] was a pleasure to work with and the assignment was right up my alley!

Here's another pitch I'd like to throw your way. When decorating a child's room, families often try to incorporate a child's interests and tastes. And though the store shelves are stocked high with themed bedding, curtains and wallpaper borders, there are some very easy ways to make your child's room special by really personalizing it. This piece could be called "Personal Best: How to really make a child's room their own" and feature a variety of ideas from framed original art work, to hand prints on the closet door, to a hand painted mural or self portrait (with a little parental guidance of course). I'd include ideas on using a child's initial throughout the room, or focusing on a child's favorite color.

In my own kids' rooms, I've painted their name on their bedroom door, made pillows using their first initial and covered their walls with their own, framed artwork. Why hide a kid's growth on a chart in the basement when you can do it right inside their closet wall or on the back of their door? I'd also include ideas for children sharing a room (mine did for six years). I think that it would be a great piece for one of your spring issues, as families are cleaning up, rearranging and sprucing up their homes.

Please let me know if you're interested in this piece as soon as possible, as I'd like to pass it along elsewhere if it doesn't fit your needs.

Thanks again,
Sharon

Canadian Broadcasting Corp. (CBC) - $2,000

George Balogh is a turkey farmer residing in Central Ontario, with a penchant for tracking con-men for investigative journalistic assignments.

~~~~~

The Fifth Estate is a Canadian investigative journalism show similar to *60 Minutes* in the U.S. It is produced by the *Canadian Broadcasting Corp. (CBC)*.

George's query letter below starts with an outstanding hook! It is immediately obvious that his idea is a great human-interest topic. Who can read the first paragraph and not want to learn more? Any editor who is intrigued by a great hook knows the writer can entertain his readers in the same way!

The second paragraph mentions celebrities and athletes. Editors (and producers) know their readers love to hear about famous people. Even if no names are mentioned, knowing some celebrities have sought help from this firm make this a great article idea.

Then comes the clincher...dirt! The author has inside knowledge of the downfall of the "hero" of this story and is offering an exclusive. The media loves to get the exclusive from insiders!

What makes George's query a hit:
1. Outstanding hook!
2. Great human-interest topic of interest to the general population.
3. Mentions celebrities and famous athletes.
4. Offers insider information and an exclusive.

After receiving George's query, the producers responded with a written letter to schedule a meeting. George Balogh was paid $2,000 for writing the treatment for the program and for serving as a consultant on the story. This query was sent via fax.

George's $2,000 Query

G. LESLIE BALOGH

(xxx) xxx-xxxx
FAX xxx-xxxx
Street Address
City, State, Zip

Date

Producer's Name
Executive Producer
FIFTH ESTATE
C.B.C. Toronto Office
Fax Number

Dear Sir,

He began as a minister—a one-time evangelist for a conservative religious denomination in Canada. A man of vision and grit—a former heavily addicted cocaine user who eventually saw the error of his way, he turned to the church as a "vehicle" to help others.

In his zeal for the "cleaned up life" he never forgot that his closest friend died of a cocaine overdose. And, after eight years of ministry, he left the salaried ministry to found Canada's most innovative drug prevention program, enlisting the voluntary assistance of hall-of-fame athletes and celebrities.

The success of his drug prevention methods harnessed the same principles he had noticed in the marketing methods of the major breweries...in reverse. And other drug education organizations were intimidated by the emotional excitement that drew school children into adopting his achievement oriented, goal-setting presentations, pointing the way to the drug-free lifestyle. He was a one-man-peer-pressure-reversal "machine"!

He recruited successful business professionals and began to expand into other regions on Canada. A prominent Southern U.S. police department sought him out and together with a Regan-appointed Drug Enforcement Officer he became the first Canadian charity to be used as a model for duplication by these agencies in a major drug racketeering center in the U.S. He was called in by government officials in the Grand Cayman Islands due to his rising fame. But that was on the way up.

Then the crunch began. He was growing too fast in Canada and had turned to the U.S. due to the overwhelming interest shown him there. Financial difficulties began to mount; he was too innovative for Canada. Then came Revenue Canada and the inkling of an investigation.

The man currently resides in the "Sunbelt" where he is running an American and Canadian version of his innovative education program—both nationally registered charities which advocate drug prevention programming as its mission to youth. He still conducts fundraising campaigns in Canada using celebrities, but has not been known to conduct major educational programming to correspond with funds raised. I should know: formerly, I was one of his chief aides.

What I am proposing to you is that the FIFTH ESTATE produce a program entitled: "The Drug Wars: Anatomy of a Charity" in which we would put into perspective the complete disclosure of the aforementioned. I am willing to negotiate your interest in this story on an exclusive basis, allowing FIFTH ESTATE to break the story first. I will be available to function in consultation as needed until airing.

Under girding the soap-opera-like interludes is the fundamental message that Canada charitable ventures are a multi-billion dollar enterprise. Thousands of private charities are registered that, presumably, believe in their charitable venture. My story is the case of one that began well but went sour due to multiple bunglings and mismanagement.

Your written confirmation by return fax as to your interest in pursuing this topic for purposes of discussion will be the first step in arranging an appointment. I am approaching FIFTH ESTATE with the first right of refusal or acceptance of this programming idea.

Yours sincerely,

George Balogh

Woman's Day - $2,000

Kathryn Lay has published 800 articles and stories in Woman's Day, Family Circle, Woman's World, Guideposts, Kiwanis, Christian Parenting Today, Cricket, and many others. Her first children's novel, King of Fifth Grade (Holiday House books) is due in bookstores soon. She teaches writing classes at Coffeehouseforwriters.com and can be reached via email at rlay15@aol.com. Kathryn's website is located at: http://hometown.aol.com/rlay15/index.html

~~~~~

Kathryn Lay's query to *Woman's Day* is simple and its target audience is broad, obviously appealing to the general population (and the audience of any mainstream women's magazine). From the very top of her letterhead, where Kathryn mentions her upcoming book as well as her affiliation with a writer's organization, the editor is assured that Kathryn is a professional, published writer.

Writers who offer flexibility (offering to meet the editor's preferred word count and deadline) are popular with editors and Kathryn's query shows she's easy to work with and able to deliver the product to the editor's specifications. Kathryn agrees to write this article at any word count and by any deadline while allowing the editor to choose which safety issues she'll cover. This can-do attitude has contributed to Kathryn's freelance writing success.

What makes Kathryn's query a hit:
1. Establishes her professional status by mentioning her book and writing organization affiliation on her letterhead.
2. Offers the editor a choice of topics to cover in the article.

3. Offers to create and deliver the article to editor's desired specs.

Woman's Day paid Kathryn $2,000 for her article.

Kathryn's $2,000 Query

Kathryn Lay
http://hometown.aol.com/rlay15/index.html
NC/NE Texas SCBWI Regional Advisor
Author of KING OF FIFTH GRADE, *Holiday House, Fall 2004*

Dear [Editor's First Name]:

Throughout our world, we are faced with safety issues in our everyday life and when we play. Knowing and preparing for these issues is the first and best step to staying safe.

"Safety-Proofing Your World" would provide readers with safety ideas on several key areas of their lives. Although some of us know or think we know the basic ways to practice safety in our everyday world, we may be caught surprised when an issue comes up and we are not prepared. I have 6 proposed topics and 3 subtopics in each area.

My information will come from experts in various fields, as well as information gleaned from official Internet sites.

Topics can include:

> Traveling without Fear (example included)
> Weathering the Storm (example included)
> Driving Safe
>> Basic Maintenance
>> Avoiding Road Rage
>> When a Breakdown Happens
> Safety-Proof Your Computer
>> From Viruses

From Child Stalkers
From Shams, Scams, and Thieves
Safety-Proof Your Child's World
   In the Car
   Stranger Danger
   On the Playground
   Home Safe Home
   Carbon Monoxide
   Security
   Surviving a Fire

I can provide "Safety-Proofing Your World" at your preferred word count and deadline date.

My writing includes 500 articles and stories in: *Woman's Day, Guideposts, Woman's World, Eckerd's I Am…Me, Home Life*, and hundreds more.

Thank you for your time. I look forward to hearing from you.

Sincerely,

Kathryn Lay

DiscoveryHealth.com - $2,000

Yocheved Golani is a generalist with a specialty in health-related writing having edited biotechnology and medical technology textbooks. Yocheved also covers topics ranging from art to biography, philosophy, religion, science, and more for a variety of authors and publishers in several print and online publications. She also publishes INK. Readers can subscribe to INK by sending a blank email to: GOGOLANI-subscribe@topica.com

Yocheved's novel, Legacy, is a fast-paced action, espionage thriller. See: http://www.booklocker.com/books/514.html

The sequel to Legacy is Legacy 2006: Integrity which tackles current events, real military concerns, a little-known group of adherents to Noachide, Bible codes, archaeology and their relationship to unfolding global history. With profound, prophetic insight regarding the Middle East, Legacy 2006: Integrity includes a "jaw-dropping" ending. See:
http://www.booklocker.com/books/1357.html

You can read more about Yocheved Golani online at: http://www.ygolani.com

~~~~~

Yocheved Golani is another tireless self-marketer, concocting unique article ideas and submitting queries with ease and professionalism. I have personally worked with Yocheved over the past two years on non-fiction articles and books as well as her novels, *Legacy* and *Legacy 2006: Integrity*.

Yocheved's query for *DiscoveryHealth.com* opens with her former yet impressive and relevant job title. She continues by alerting the editor to her vast medical writing experience, but also notes that she can write for the non-medical community (consumers) with ease. She also offers examples from her current files in the event the editor requires further documentation of her expertise in the medical writing field.

I encourage you to visit Yocheved's very impressive website at the link above to see how she markets herself to editors online.

What makes Yocheved's query a hit:
1. Former title shows she's perfect for this particular job.
2. Mentions her contacts in the medical field.
3. Mentions she can write medical content in layman's terms (for the general public).
4. Provides link to her professional, well designed website.

This query was sent via email. *DiscoveryHealth.com* paid Yocheved $2,000 for her article.

Yocheved's $2,000 Query

Dear Mr. [Editor's Last Name],

As a former Health Information Management professional, I often write feature stories pertaining to health and medicine. My excellent resources within the medical world and lively writing style enable me to offer cutting-edge material that educates lay readers in an entertaining fashion.

I propose to write a feature about advances in a previously and dangerously overlooked population: women with cardiac problems. Emergency rooms and family doctors often dismiss the signs and symptoms of serious heart disease in women, even as they suffer heart attacks in front of these professionals. I have ample material and case histories to present in my work.

I invite you to visit my website for an overview of my capabilities. I look forward to your response.

Yocheved Golani
http://www.ygolani.com

Chemical Innovation - $2,200

Pauline Hamilton is a qualified pharmacist who launched a full-time freelance writing career from her home in New Zealand in 2000. She specializes in pharmaceutical and biotechnology subjects. Her writing credits include articles in Chemical Innovations, Drug and Market Developments Newsletter, Pharmacy Today, and the New Zealand Pharmacy Magazine. You can reach Pauline via her website at:
http://PHamilton.globaltelecommute.com

~~~~~

In her query to *Chemical Innovation* below, Pauline Hamilton casually mentions her professional experience (she's a pharmacist) and in the very next sentence boldly states that she is a freelancer working from home while she raises her two young children. While this might bring sympathy from some editors, it is more likely to scare editors away. Some may consider this statement a sign of a work-at-home mom rather than a professional writer. However, Pauline reassures the editor of her professional status by sharing information about her current, impressive assignment. We quickly realize this is no part-time writer/full-time mom!

Pauline also includes a copy of an article (writing sample) and a link to her online résumé, which you can view at: http://phamilton.globaltelecommute.com

Pauline admits, "As you will see, it is a query which breaks just about every rule in the 'how to write a successful query' rule book (if such a thing exists), but was still successful. In the issue where my article was published, the editor actually made mention of my personal circumstances."

Yes, Pauline sent email attachments without asking first, which is a big taboo in the online community. But, it obviously didn't scare this editor away.

What makes Pauline's query a hit:
1. Is honest about her working conditions but mentions current, impressive contract.
2. Doesn't waste the editor's time; makes her pitch quickly and succinctly.

Chemical Innovation paid Pauline $2,200 for her article, which was published as a cover story. Unfortunately, the publication is now defunct. Her query was sent via email.

Pauline's $2,200 Query

From: Pauline Hamilton
Sent: Wednesday, May 02 7:31 PM
Subject: freelance articles

Hi [Editor's First Name],

I am a pharmacist living in New Zealand. I am looking primarily for freelance work from my home as I have two young children to care for.

I am, at present, writing articles on R&D in therapeutic groups for an American company, and have just completed an editing contract for an Auckland based firm (all work was completed off-site, via phone and email as I am based in Oamaru, in the South Island of New Zealand).

I have attached my résumé and two writing examples for your perusal.

I would like to write an article(s) for you outlining in further depths the research and developments occurring in the New Zealand biotech industry.

I look forward to hearing from you,

Many Thanks
Pauline Hamilton Dip. Pharm MPS

Lifetime Magazine - $3,000

Melissa Walker is a writer and magazine editor living in Brooklyn.

~~~~~

Melissa Walker's short, informal email query, along with a subsequent, more detailed query letter, appear below. Melissa's tone is informal and enthusiastic in her introduction, yet her information is professional and succinctly detailed in the informal query paragraph. And, as stated earlier, any query that mentions celebrities is usually a big hit with editors!

Her formal query below reads like an article and you are quickly drawn into the subject's plight. With this outstanding talent for keeping the reader (in this case, the editor) in suspense, the editor knew Melissa will offer the same tasty morsel for their readers.

What makes Melissa's query a hit:
1. Offers four possible article titles.
2. Great suspense!
3. Query reads like an article, not like a query letter.
4. Mentions celebrities.

Lifetime Magazine paid Melissa $3,000 for her article. Both queries appearing below were sent via email.

Melissa's Informal Query

Hi, [Editor's First Name].

I sent some clips last week, and I have an idea. Let me know i
you think it might work—or if you have something smaller yo
want to try me out on. I'd love to write something for you!

For Real Lives, Real Women, stuntwoman Dana Hee, 36, woul(
make an amazing profile. The piece would focus on Dana's job a:
a stuntperson, including funny and thrilling experiences she's ha(
working on Hollywood sets. She has been a stand-in for Nicol(
Kidman, Gwyneth Paltrow, Cameron Diaz and more, and sh(
currently works as Jennifer Garner's stunt double on the hit sho\
"Alias." Dana overcame abuse, abandonment and alcoholisn
during her childhood, and as she learned to strengthen her body
she also strengthened her mind—she's a motivational speaker ir
her spare time. I think this story would work best as an "as told to
so that Dana's descriptions of action are immediate.

Melissa's Formal $3,000 Query

Possible display copy:

From Nerd to the Hollywood Herd
Stuntwoman Dana Hee kicks ass—moviestar style

Would Cameron Diaz lunch with a nerd? Stuntwoman an(
former high school outcast Dana Hee says yes.

Hee-Woman
Stunt double Dana Hee takes the heat for Hollywood's A-list starlets

Cinderella with a Kick
Stuntwoman Dana Hee went from high school nerd to the Hollywood Herd

Thirty-six-year-old Dana Hee has lived a Cinderella story that makes fairy tales look like child's play. The former "reject" takes stunt hits for A-list movie stars—and then she joins them for lunch.

Growing up in Baton Rouge, Louisiana, Dana's life read like a movie script, but there was no Hollywood ending in sight. When she was three, Dana's parents—both alcoholics—divorced, and Dana and her two older brothers were placed in an orphanage. Eight years later, her father (who did not have legal custody) kidnapped the three kids and brought them to California. Alcoholism, abandonment and abduction led Dana into the courtroom when her mother filed a bitter custody suit. The children had to choose which parent they would live with, and they chose their mom.

But Dana was hiding a secret. Her stepfather had been sexually molesting her during visits since she was six years old. With no end in sight to this abuse or to her mother's alcoholic rages, Dana ran away from home at age 14. She was picked up by authorities and shuttled between halfway houses, government shelters and then a foster family.

In high school, Dana was quiet and unpopular—she felt alienated by the grief of her overwhelming past, and she never made many friends. Only one part of her life brought her any relief—she excelled at track and field. As Dana's feet pounded on the ground, she could feel the anger and sadness flowing out of her. A hunger for healing drove her to new athletic heights, and when Dana enrolled in junior college, she took up Taekwando.

In Taekwando class, Dana met her future husband. By 21, she was a housewife by day, and Dana thought she'd finally found the love she needed. But at night, she was still training while her husband dozed to Monday Night Football. The marriage didn't last; Dana spent more and more time at the gym, and her husband wanted a wife at home. They divorced after six years.

Dana's intensity with the weight machines not only helped her release the pain of her past, it also led her to the ultimate athletic competition: the Olympics. In 1988, Dana struck gold in Seoul for her Taekwando prowess. Then the party really started.

In the summer of 1991, Dana got a phone call from Hollywood saying they needed someone with martial arts skills to do some stunt work. Her response: "What should I pack?"

Once the shy girl in high school, Dana's rolodex now reads like a Hollywood Who's Who, and after 12 years of doubling for Hollywood starlets, she has tales to tell. "The good news is that there are some darlings among the divas," Dana says. Working with Cameron Diaz in "Gangs of New York," Dana found the actress to be a consummate professional—and a great lunch buddy. Cameron worked in the bitter cold weather despite a fever and chills, and she often rested over a bite to eat with Dana and some other cast members at a local Italian diner. They all laughed and joked together—gabbing like old friends (albeit famous ones) about everything from a cute cameraman to diet tips. Dana says that Cameron is "truly a woman of class and heart who deserves all the recognition she's gotten." Then she adds, "I just wish they all were like her!"

The devilish divas in the pack include Geena Davis, who didn't want anyone to know she wasn't doing her own stunts for "The

Long Kiss Goodnight" (yeah right, Geena). Dana spent five hours each morning getting into a prosthetic Geena mask each day—even the crew didn't know! And B-lister Penelope Anne Miller was even more insecure than Geena, Dana reports. She didn't want other women on the set of "The Shadow," so Dana ducked around corners whenever the actress appeared. "She even got a stand-in fired for talking with men on the set!" says Dana.

From a cowering, abused little girl, Dana has reinvented herself as a Hollywood insider who attends tea parties at Ben Kingsley's chateau and cracks jokes with John Travolta between movie takes. Still in her 30s, Dana is younger than lots of leading actresses (yes, Meg Ryan, Jodie Foster and Madonna are all 40-something), and she plans to keep working it as long as they do. Plus, Dana's just becoming a red-carpet regular—she won her first Taurus Award last year (the Oscar of the stunt industry). Even if the photographers snapping her picture don't recognize her face, it's not so bad when they say, "Hey! Isn't that Cameron Diaz's butt?!"

I think this story would work as either an "as told to" or as a regular feature—Dana is incredibly open about her past (less so about Hollywood stories, but we'll get some juicy tidbits like the ones above). What do you think?

Jugglezine.com - $2,000

Melanie Bowden is a freelance writer, postpartum doula, and mother of two. She has written articles for several magazines and websites including Shape Magazine, Catholic Digest, ePregnancy.com, Freelance Writer's Report, and many others. She is also the creator of the workshop, "How To Reduce New Parent Stress." Currently Melanie is working on a book titled Honest Mothers: Women Tell the Truth about Postpartum. Melanie can be reached via email at: melaniebowden@earthlink.net

~~~~~

Melanie Bowden's successful query below was sent as an informal email. Her first sentence lets the editor know that at least one-third of their readers will be interested in this article. She then offers to share information she has learned from a doctor (professional advice) and that she has personal experience with the topic as well. She then offers to share information from yet another doctor as well as an author (more professional advice) and shows she's done her homework by sharing that she's already lined up interviews for this article.

What makes Melanie's query a hit:
1. General interest topic (large target audience for this article).
2. Licensed professionals and a published author have already committed to interviews for the article.
3. Writer has personal experience with the topic.

Jugglezine.com paid Melanie $2,000 for her article. This query was sent via email.

Melanie's $2,000 Query

Dear [Editor's First Name],

Did you know that 1 out of 3 American adults suffers from insomnia? In school we learn about how to eat properly and exercise, but no one teaches us how to get the best night's sleep. No wonder so many adults are stumbling through the day tired then falling into bed worried that, again, they won't get the sleep they need. I would like to write an article for Jugglezine that will show your readers how they can sleep better. The article will include information on what steps people can take to improve the quality of their sleep, whether or not they should use sleep aids, and what to do if you or your partner snores and disrupts the sleep in your household.

I recently attended a lecture by Dr. William Dement, M.D., the director of Stanford University's Sleep Disorders Clinic and Research Center and the author of "The Promise of Sleep." His suggestions have already made a difference in the quality of my sleep, and I've suffered from insomnia for years.

I could also include information on Sleep Thinking, a technique developed by Eric Maisel, Ph.D. Dr. Maisel claims that your brain is designed to think and solve problems while you sleep, without the distractions of day-to-day life. He's found that people who use his program reduce stress and increase their creativity while they sleep.

Dr. Maisel has already committed to an interview with me once the article is assigned. Author Barbara L. Heller has also agreed to an interview. Her book *"How To Sleep Soundly Tonight"* will be published in March and contains 250 tips on changing the habits that hinder sleep. The estimated word count for this article is 1,500, and I can deliver a manuscript in eight weeks.

Thank you for your consideration, [Editor's First Name].

 I look forward to your feedback on this article idea.

Sincerely,
Melanie Bowden

Unique Opportunities: The Physician's Resource - $2,550

Cindy Murphy McMahon is a writer and editor based in Omaha, Nebraska. She holds a bachelor's degree in journalism from Creighton University and a master's from the University of Missouri-Columbia School of Journalism. She specializes in health, business, and feature writing for newspapers, magazines, and online publications. Cindy and her husband, Tom, who is also a writer, have three sons.

~~~~~

Cindy Murphy McMahon had already written for *Unique Opportunities* when she sent the following informal email query to the editor. *Unique Opportunities* is a business publication for physicians.

Cindy's query offers an old topic, but with a new twist. Cindy cleverly calls her article a "primer", thus making the old topic seem new again. This is a great idea for some of those old articles floating around in your drawer that may be worth some reprint money! There are, of course, updates that should be added to old articles, but updating is often easier than starting over.

Cindy shows her flexibility by offering to meet the editor's word-count specifications. And, her query is short and uncomplicated, making it a fast read (which resulted in a fast decision and order from the editor).

What makes Cindy's query a hit:
1. Calls coverage of an old topic a primer.
2. Short, succinct query.
3. Offers to meet editor's word count requirements.

Unique Opportunities paid Cindy $2,550 for her article. This query was sent via email.

Cindy's Query

Is E-Mail the Way To Go?

I propose an update, or primer, for your readers on the legal rules, ethical guidelines and professional etiquette of using e-mail between physicians and patients.

The use of electronic communication in medical practices is growing steadily, but many physicians still have questions about security and privacy, even while they like the idea of making fewer phone calls. My sources for the article would include medical liability carriers, physician-users of e-mail in medical practice, and proponents and opponents of the trend. The technology of online communications introduces special concerns and risks that would be outlined for your readers.

The story could be as long or as short as your editorial needs dictate. I look forward to hearing from you.

Sincerely,
Cindy Murphy McMahon

A technology magazine - $8,000

K. Daniel (Danny) Glover has been covering politics and policy issues in Washington for more than a decade and is currently the managing editor of National Journal's Technology Daily, an online newsletter that covers issues affecting the technology industry. Danny was previously the associate editor of the opinion e-zine IntellectualCapital.com, where he wrote about technology, healthcare, and family issues, and authored a monthly column on congressional history. He also worked as a reporter and editor at Congressional Quarterly in Washington for almost seven years. Glover's newspaper experience includes stints at two West Virginia newspapers and The Tampa Tribune. He has been an occasional freelance writer and editor since 1996.

~~~~~

Danny Glover can't publish the name of his client for this assignment, so we have removed identifying data from the information he submitted to us. However, he has shared the editor's responses to his queries with us below.

It's obvious from his background information that Danny has a great deal of political journalism experience. His article idea is excellent and the editor knew Danny was the perfect writer for this assignment.

Danny's follow-up query below occurred after initial correspondence concerning another article idea. It's always a good idea to send a new query to an editor who has treated you with respect in the past. If an editor is writing and/or speaking to you on an informal level, keep that relationship evolving by sending another query letter, or even a short list of article ideas. If they bite, great. If they start to get cold, back off.

In the editor's response, the deal almost falls through due to timing. But, Danny gives the editor a choice – a shorter article delivered by his due date, or a more detailed, longer (worth more money) article later. The editor appreciates Danny's flexibility and opts for the long piece to run later...and even orders a second article to complement the first!

What makes Danny's query a hit:
1. Quite simply, it's a great idea that is perfect for this publication's readers! A professional, yet potentially controversial, topic is hard to pass up.
2. Danny is familiar with industry publications and mentions that the publication's competitors will likely ignore the topic.
3. Danny makes it obvious he is the perfect writer for this assignment.
4. Boldly, yet subtly, plants the idea of "cover story" in the editor's mind.

Danny was paid $4,000 for his first article...and $4,000 more for the second! This query was sent via email.

Danny's $8,000 Query Letter

[Editor's First Name],

I also wanted to pitch another story idea to you, one that I think has cover potential or that certainly could be a full-length feature The topic: Clinton's high-tech legacy.

He is our nation's first Information Age President, and he has made technology issues (the e-rate, the recently announced firstgov.gov website, the digital divide, privacy, Internet taxation) a cornerstone of his administration. He also created the first White House Website (recently redesigned) and conducted the first online "town hall" meeting.

But has he done enough? Has he accomplished all of his goals? Will history remember him for his technological milestones / successes (squashing the Y2K bug?) or his shortcomings? Will much-maligned programs like the FBI's "Carnivore" e-mail snooping system (the subject of a Hill hearing this week) tarnish his legacy?

Clinton's last year in office has been all about legacy, and I think it would be interesting to examine this one piece of his legacy, one that other publications are likely to ignore, in depth. I think it would be a great cover story sometime after the election but before Clinton leaves office.

What do you think? If you like the idea, I could start working on it right away for publication sometime down the road. (Actually, I've already done quite a bit of research on the topic.) At any rate, thanks for listening. Get back to me when you get a chance on the VC story. Thanks.

Danny

Editor's Response

Danny,

I think it's a great story, and I'd love to have you do it. Thank you for pitching it to us. How many words are you thinking (I'm negotiable) -- 2,500? I'd pay $1.00 per word.

Here's the conundrum, however. The deadline for the November issue is Sept. 1 (can be pushed to the wire of the 10th). We don't publish a regular issue again after than until February because the December/January issue is combined and the annual 100 top movers and shakers in S.A. So, I'm not sure if you could turn it around on such short notice, particularly since I waited a while to respond.

Let me know what your situation looks like and we'll figure something out.

[Editor]

Danny's Follow-up

[Editor's First Name],

If I could get lawmakers and/or Clinton but not in the short term would you be interested in running the story just after Clinton's presidency?

I could always narrow my focus or dedicate less space to each issue, but I think as broad a piece as possible is better in this case. My aim is to help SAR set the framework for future examinations of the Clinton high-tech legacy.

Danny

Editor's Follow-up

Danny,

Yes, I'd rather run it with all the information. I think we can do it in retrospect (February), even though before he left office would be preferable. I'd rather have this story be everything you envision and have all the pieces, and run it in February than just do a partial piece. Keep in touch with me, I can flex on this pretty easily between the November and February issues. For example, if you thought it was coming together by the 15th of September I could maneuver some things around to get it in (particularly since you're writing and facts are clean). If no, we can hold it off, too.

More words is fine, just didn't know what you had in mind. Shoot in the 3,000 to 4,000-word range.

Would also be interested in the next admin piece, too. In some ways this could be a two-part series. A retrospect on Clinton and then a look ahead at xxxx. If we did Clinton in Feb. we'd do xxxx in March. Let me know what you think of that.

[Editor]

Health Magazine - $2,000

Joe Mullich, a freelance writer in Sherman Oaks, California, has written for more than 100 national and regional publications. His humor writing has earned awards from the National Society of Newspaper Columnists, National Headliners, the International Society of Weekly Newspaper Editors, and others.

~~~~~

Joe Mullich initially contacted *Health Magazine* with a form pitch letter offering his bio and asking for assignments. They responded by asking him to send some articles ideas.

The circumstances in this assignment are a bit unusual. Joe said, "I sent an email with a bunch of one-paragraph story ideas to *Health Magazine*. I didn't know any editors over there and they didn't know me. My ideas found their way to one of their many editors who needed a story quick (two week deadline) - I think something had fallen through on her. (The idea below) is what she picked from about a dozen items (in my query)."

Joe admits his "wordsmithing" in the query reads in an awkward fashion, but says he sends queries out quickly. "I like to dash them off, reducing the amount of speculative writing I do to a minimum. I guess it just hit the right person at the right time."

He adds, "She assigned a 1000-word piece for $2,000, and then asked, 'Oh, you have written for magazines before?' (The ideas had been funneled to her through another editor who hadn't shared my clips with her, so I think she assumed I'd already been vetted -- buy maybe not.) Subsequently, the editors decided to combine a couple of the other story pitches on the list into one article and assigned it to me for about $4,000. This all started in March. Got two more assignments from them since then, so that initial letter paid some good dividends. I am a big advocate of the scattershot approach -- sending a bunch of small items in one letter. Editors seem to like choices and, if they see you have good ideas, they are quite willing to hone those ideas with you. My three subsequent assignments, while based on my pitches, had their slant significantly changed after discussions with the editors."

While Joe took a chance by sending a list of ideas rather than one query letter, his approach paid off. Some editors prefer to review a list of article ideas rather than one-query-at-a-time.

What makes Joe's query a hit:
1. Pitches multiple article ideas in one-paragraph-per-idea format.
2. Offers to work with the editor to hone the article ideas to fit their needs.

Health Magazine paid Joe $2,000 for his first article. The initial query (list of article ideas) ultimately earned him thousands more. This query was sent via email.

Joe's $2,000 Query

Keep your pantry trans-fat free: Within the next few months the FDA is going to require all packaged food to list the amount of trans fat it contains. Trans fat has been shown in studies to be even more harmful to one's body than saturated fat. Consumption not only raises bad cholesterol, but also decreases good cholesterol. Trans fat comes in some surprising sources, including some breakfast cereals. How about telling readers how to avoid feeding their families trans fat by telling them what to look for, what to avoid, and how to read the labels?

Woman's Day - $2,800

Kelly James-Enger escaped from the law in 1997. Since then, the former attorney's work has appeared in more than 45 national magazines, including Redbook, Woman's Day, Family Circle, and Self. She's a contributing editor for Oxygen, Energy for Women, Complete Woman, For the Bride, and The Writer. She specializes in health, fitness, and nutrition subjects and is the author of Ready, Aim, Specialize! Create Your Own Writing Specialty and Make More Money (The Writer Books, 2003) and the novels, Did You Get the Vibe? (Kensington Books, November, 2003) and White Bikini Panties (Kensington Books, 2004). Read more about Kelly online at: http://www.kellyjamesenger.com

~~~~~

Kelly James-Enger directly approached the health director at *Woman's Day* for her article idea. Kelly's first sentence in her query letter is a statement any woman can relate to and, using first person, Kelly pulls the reader into the query on a personal level. If you're a woman, you can't help yourself. You simply must keep reading what Kelly has to say. Kelly obviously has a talent for suspense.

Upon reading the second paragraph, you think...yeah, she's right! I DO eat more chocolate, LOTS of it, when I'm depressed! Kelly is still pulling the reader along on a personal level, and she hasn't even written the article yet!

Kelly then provides additional article information and offers to interview experts to help us, including the spokesperson for the American Dietetic Association (experts validate the facts presented!).

Finally, Kelly even identifies the specific section of the magazine that the article would complement, making it easy for the editor to envision exactly where that article would fit her editorial needs.

What makes Kelly's query a hit:
1. Great suspense! Makes you want to keep reading!
2. Covers a topic that almost every woman can relate to.
3. Uses first-person to pull the reader in on a personal level.
4. Offers expert advice from licensed professionals.
5. Recommends magazine section for the article.

Woman's Day paid $2,800 for Kelly's article. Kelly already had a working relationship with the editor, so she sent this informal query via email.

Kelly's $2,800 Query

Dear [Editor's First Name]:

You'd noticed that your pants were getting a little snug, but didn't think anything of it. It wasn't until you slipped into your favorite skirt—and could barely button it—that you forced yourself onto the scale, only to discover you'd gained eight pounds. But you haven't changed your eating or exercise habits, so why are you gaining weight?

Guess what? Those extra pounds may be a symptom of depression or anxiety. A recently published survey found that the more psychologically stressed women were, the more calories they consumed and the fewer fruits and vegetables they ate. Women who said they were stressed were also more than twice as likely to binge eat.

Your weight gain may also be the result of eating a lot of high-glycemic foods, which enter the bloodstream quickly. Research suggests that a high-glycemic diet may lead to more frequent feelings of hunger and lead to weight gain while eating lower-glycemic foods can help dieters lose or maintain their weight. Other weight gain culprits include frequent dining out—a recent study found that the portions of foods like hamburgers and French fries are two to five times larger than the original versions. It's easy to "supersize" without thinking about the additional calories. Mindless snacking in front of the television, being unaware of the portions you usually eat, a natural loss in muscle mass that occurs as we grow older, and less frequent exercise can all result in a slow but steady weight gain.

Identify and combat these "hidden" influences, and you'll find it easier to lose weight as well as prevent weight gain in your 30s and 40s. "Is your Life Making you Fat? Get Slim—and Stay that Way" will show readers how to uncover and overcome these factors in their own lives. I'll interview experts such as Epel and American Dietetic Association spokesperson Roxanne Moore R.D. for this story; a possible sidebar might include "Sneaky Fitness Tips", a list of ways to increase your amount of daily activity. While I estimate 1500 words for this story, that's flexible depending on your needs.

Donna, let me know if you're interested in this story for your "Diet/Exercise" section or if you have any questions about it—otherwise I'll follow up on it in a couple of weeks.

As always, thanks for your time.

Best,
Kelly

Redbook - $3,500

Kelly James-Enger's bio can be read in the preceding chapter.

~~~~~

As with the query in the previous chapter, Kelly James-Enger again shows her talent for capturing the attention of women! The editor reading the query below knows the vast majority of her readers suffer from this condition (PMS) and any new medical ideas to alleviate it would be warmly embraced by her readers.

Kelly proceeds to introduce experts, (to validate her statements) and shows she's done her research by introducing manufacturers who are producing new medicines to help.

You'll also notice that Kelly has quite a talent for titles. I doubt many editors change the catchy ones she concocts. She concludes by stating her qualifications, which are quite impressive (and include many of *Redbook's* competitors).

What makes Kelly's query a hit:
1. Again, great suspense. Women want to keep reading to see how they, too, can eliminate this problem.
2. Has located experts to validate claims.
3. Mentions manufacturers already working on new technology (shows she's done her homework).
4. Very professional, clean, well-written query.
5. Includes clips from the publication's major competitors.

Redbook paid Kelly $3,500 for her article. This query was sent via regular mail with photocopies of Kelly's clips.

Kelly's $2,500 Query

Date

Editor's Full Name
Senior Editor, Health
Redbook
Mailing Address
City, State, Zip

Dear Mrs. [Editor's Last Name]:

Swollen, tender breasts. Headaches. Irritability. Depression According to the American College of Obstetricians and Gynecologists, 85% of menstruating women experience one o more premenstrual symptoms every month, and most experience cramps ranging from mild to debilitating during their periods as well.

But researchers are suggesting that this monthly discomfort is unnecessary—and that it may in fact be healthier to have fewer menstrual periods. According to scientist Sheldon Segal, author o *Is Menstruation Obsolete?* (Oxford University Press, 1999), having fewer periods reduces pre-menstrual syndrome and eliminates discomfort associated with endometriosis while protecting women against iron-deficiency anemia. Barr Laboratories is currently developing Seasonale, an oral contraceptive that will produce only 4 menstrual periods a year, and hopes to have it available by 2003. Another pharmaceutical company is working on a nasal contraceptive that will contain fewer hormones than birth control pills and will produce 3-month menstrual cycles. Could monthly periods soon be a thing of the past?

"Your Monthly Period: Necessity or Nuisance?" will examine the question of whether longer menstrual cycles (e.g., having a period every 3 months instead of every month) are healthier for women and explore the research and theories behind this novel concept. I'll interview nationally-recognized women's health experts to include the possible pros and cons of "skipping" periods and will report on current research and new products being developed. While I estimate 2,000 words for this in-depth story, that's flexible depending on your needs.

Interested in this story for your "Health & Fitness" section? I'm a full-time freelancer whose health stories have appeared in magazines including *Family Circle, Cosmopolitan, Woman's Day, Marie Claire, Fitness,* and *Shape;* clips are enclosed. If you have any questions about this story idea, please let me know.

Thank you for your time; I look forward to hearing from you soon.

Very truly yours,

Kelly James-Enger

Xephon / Insight IS - $2,150 + $40,000 over four years

Murdoch Mactaggart has been a freelance writer since mid-199?, following earlier periods as a printer and publisher, an antiquarian bookseller and dealer in original prints, a software developer, and a computer consultant. He has a degree in political science and sought unsuccessfully on more than one occasion to be elected to both the European and UK parliaments.

Much of his current writing is in the specialist areas of computing and mobile telecomms but he also writes articles in diverse areas such as business issues, government and politics, art, and science, particularly on future developments. He plays tennis, a touch obsessively according to some, and seeks to balance this dubious interest in physical exercise with strong consumer support for the French, Italian, and South American red wine industries, and by cooking decent food.

His four children have all long since left home and are variously involved in film, music, design, conservation, or wine. He lives in west Dorset, UK, and sometimes in the west highlands of Scotland near Skye. Murdoch can be reached via email at ww@textbiz.com

~~~~~

The query below was Murdoch Mactaggart's initial approach to *Insight IS* after being referred to the publication by one of the editor's colleagues. The informational query, sent via email, turned into a very lucrative, long-term relationship.

Murdoch said, "The email copied below was written towards the end of 1998 and was my first approach to the editor of *Xephon's* flagship publication, *Insight IS*. I had been a freelance writer for about a year and had already written for one of *Xephon's* other publications. That editor suggesting I approach his colleague. The immediate result of the letter was a commission to write an article on the European Single Currency (see paragraph 3) and invoiced at £1,320, or approximately $2,150."

Murdoch's query begins with the admission that he may not be qualified to write about some of the topics covered by the magazine. Most editors easily recognize boastfulness and inflated qualifications, so Murdoch's honesty is no-doubt appreciated by the editor. Editors, like all people, prefer working with honest, humble professionals rather than narcissistic ones that push the truth to the limit and beyond. And, despite his lack of knowledge in some aspects of their coverage, Murdoch quickly shows his expertise in others.

What makes Murdoch's query a hit:
1. Honest, not boastful.
2. Drops a name (the editor's colleague) and offers him as a reference later in the query.
3. Professional, succinct, and well-written.

After the initial assignment, Murdoch continued to write for *Insight IS* and to contribute to *Xephon's* reports and conferences until the company ceased those activities late last year. His initial query below resulted in his first assignment of $2,150, and assignments totaling $40,000 over the following four years.

Murdoch's $2,150+ Query

[Editor's First Name],

[Editor's Colleague's Name], for whom I'm written a fair amount, gave me a copy of Insight IS and suggested that I look at it from the point of view of perhaps offering articles to you. I've now read through the magazine and although there's rather more of an emphasis on larger systems than I might know about I think there could be some overlap between my areas of experience and what you need for your readership.

I've been involved with business for over thirty years and with computers for approaching twenty. Most of my experience is with smaller machines, PCs particularly, and with small businesses. For the past few years I've acted principally as an IT consultant although I've also written a fair amount of software. For around a year now I've been contributing articles to various publications - Web Update, PCSA, PCNA, PC Week, IT Week, Internet.Works, Network Solutions, Application Development Advisor, Component Strategies, and others - and this is now my main work activity. I'm familiar with a number of areas of IT from a technical perspective, with management and related issues from a business perspective, and with political and especially European Union matters.

One subject area which may be of interest to you in the form of an in depth review (as per the Y2K article in your September issue) is that of the European single currency. This is, as I'm sure you're aware, a much misunderstood issue which is a strategic one with significant IT implications. EMU is something I do know a fair amount about and I'd be happy to discuss with you the outlines of an article if that's of interest.

If you'd like to see examples of what I've written or to get more information about what I do write then I'll be happy to send some files to you. [Editor's Colleague's Name] can, no doubt, also be approached.

Regards

Murdoch Mactaggart

Oracle - $2,500

Murdoch Mactaggart's bio appears in the preceding chapter.

~~~~~

Oracle, one of the largest software companies in the world, has headquarters in Redwood Shores, California. While at an *Oracle* event in Copenhagen, Murdoch Mactaggart approached a senior *Oracle* executive about writing for the company's developer website. The executive passed Murdoch's name on to an *Oracle* editor who contacted him and asked for background details.

Murdoch said, "My email was passed on by its recipient to a section editor who then commissioned me to write an article worth $2,500 around the interview mentioned near the end of my email." The story appeared last September and is currently accessible at: http://otn.oracle.com/oramag/webcolumns/2002/opinion/secure_d avidson01.html

Murdoch's first positive action in getting this assignment was not hesitating to introduce himself to an editor at an event. Things fell into place via email after that.

Murdoch adds, "In this particular case, I've left the email intact because it covers the three areas of personal background, writing samples and feature suggestions, the first two typically requested by a new editorial contact. The feature suggestion inclusion was on my initiative and not something requested by the editor."

Murdoch answers the editor's email directly in the body of the email while leaving the editor's original note in the reply (so as not to confuse the editor) and pastes the requested information in the body of the email, too. Murdoch includes his bio, a paragraph connecting his experience directly to their needs (and an offer to mail a clip that complement's *Oracle's* needs, links to six online "clips" complete with brief article descriptions, and, finally, his actual query.

What makes Murdoch's query a hit:
1. Professional yet friendly.
2. Leaves email intact to alleviate confusion for the editor.
3. Pastes CV (bio) into body of the email and ensures formatting is simple and attractive.
4. Provides links to online clips (rather than sending attachments) along with article descriptions (in case the editor doesn't want to or doesn't have time to click).
5. Pitches a feature article idea even though the editor didn't ask for one.

The email correspondence is shown exactly as it was sent, but we have offset the editor's original email with italics. *Oracle* paid Murdoch $2,500 for his article.

Murdoch's Response to Editor's Email

Hi Murdoch,

I'm [Name], the editor of Oracle Magazine. [Executive's Name] gave me your name as a possible contributor to the magazine (the two of you met at OracleWorld in Copenhagen).

Thanks for the email. Yes, Rene and I spoke after one of his presentations and said that he would ask you and a colleague from OTN to be in touch.

Could you tell me a bit about yourself, your areas of expertise, and point me to writing samples?

Sure. Firstly, here are a couple of paragraphs from a mini-cv which I generally send out as background information.

In addition to the information you asked for, I've included at the end a couple of feature suggestions deriving from meetings interviews at the recent event in Denmark.

Murdoch Mactaggart is a freelance writer, presenter and occasional consultant concentrating particularly in the area of information technology (IT). He's been involved with IT for over twenty years in areas ranging from business analysis through software specification and development, consulting and independent importing and retailing. He's developed software using mechanisms ranging from machine code through to VB, C++, Java and specialist web application development tools.

He writes principally in the areas of software development and technologies, security and cryptography, the Internet and eBusiness, and European Union issues such as the single European currency. Many of his articles are aimed at explaining technology from a business-related perspective or connecting together technology, business and politics/economics issues.

Publications for which he's written recently include Application Development Advisor, MIS UK, Reach, British Computer Society Bulletin, IT Week, Computer Weekly, IBM developerWorks, Component Strategies, and specialist subscription journals such as Insight IS, Oracle Update, NT Update, PC Support Advisor and PC Network Advisor. He's recently supplied specialist features for periodicals published for Price Waterhouse Coopers, The Chartered Institute of Marketing, the British Quality Foundation, IATA, and others. In addition to writing features, Murdoch Mactaggart writes both technical and business related white papers, in-depth analyses and case studies, and marketing collateral for IT industry use.

I've been a full time freelance features writer for approaching five years. Many of my articles take an in-depth approach being either for developers (as for Application Development Advisor or IBM developerWorks) or for IT professionals with limited specialist technical knowledge and which seek to explain the relevance of particular technologies with a business/management/strategy emphasis (as for Insight IS, MIS UK, PCSA, PCNA, Computer Weekly, IT Week etc.) Other features are generally shorter, aimed at business managers and others who may have little IT technical understanding but who need to understand the implications of IT in particular areas (as for Reach, IATA, CIM, BQF, etc.) I write particularly on cryptography, more generally on security, on the Internet and on associated technologies such as XML or web services, on software development issues and on more peripheral matters such as copyright and patents, nanotechnology, and generally "interesting" areas of that type, particularly where social issues may be involved (my degree is in Politics/Philosophy and used to be active in politics).

WRITING SAMPLES

Most of my articles on the web tend to be technical in nature so what follows is a bit thin in other areas. However, I can always mail examples to you if what I've pointed to here isn't adequate. wrote a couple of white papers for Oracle UK two or three years ago but they don't seem to be web-accessible any more, although I could always mail a copy if you want.

This was written following my attending Oracle Open World 2001 in Berlin and looks at Oracle's developer strategies. It appeared in Application Development Advisor:
http://www.appdevadvisor.co.uk/Downloads/ada5_8/Oracle'sTies. pdf

This is another ADA article, looking at Java on non-PC platforms http://www.appdevadvisor.co.uk/Downloads/ada5_4/SizeIsn't5_4. pdf

The following general feature, a look at the multimedia product from the Shoah foundation, appeared in Computer Weekly a couple of years' back:
http://www.findarticles.com/cf_0/m0COW/2000_April_20/6211576 5/p1/article.jhtml

This is a fairly technical article on security related XML standards developments, published last autumn in IBM developerWorks:
http://www-106.ibm.com/developerworks/security/library/s-xmlsec.html

This feature on XML and web services was published last December in Reach, a European wide quarterly periodical for business managers and sponsored by Microsoft, Intel and some smaller IT companies:

http://www.onwindows.com/features/xmlwebservices.htm

The following feature, on Bayesian Theory, was published recently in the Bulletin of the British Computer Society:
http://www.bcs.org.uk/publicat/ebull/mar02/leading.htm

FEATURE SUGGESTIONS
BAE Systems and Oracle 9iAS
BAE Systems, based in the UK, is the world's second largest defence company. Over the past year or a little longer one of its sections, formed specifically to oversee the project of building type 45 anti-aircraft destroyers for the Royal Navy, has grown hugely in size and has managed the issue of sharing information among the different subsections by implementing Oracle 91 AS and specifically the portal facilities therein. I interviewed the Information Systems and Solutions Manager for the project who spoke very enthusiastically about his team's experiences with the software and how it facilitated greatly the sharing of information at different levels in ways which they had found impossible earlier. You may, therefore, be interested in a case study or similar type of feature written around this project and its challenges.

Oracle and security issues
I also attended a session by and later interviewed on a one to one basis Mary Ann Davidson, Oracle's CSO. Given the growing importance attached to security and the focus Oracle is placing on this you may be interested in running an edited version of that interview or else in a feature drawing heavily on what she discussed with me.

Thanks again for contacting me. I look forward to hearing from you again shortly and, subject to the conditions and terms on which Oracle Magazine works with freelances, perhaps writing for you.

Should you want to discuss anything by phone, incidentally, m‹ number is +44+xxx…

Regards
Murdoch Mactaggart
Email Address

IBM developer website - $15,000

*Murdoch Mactaggart's bio appears in the preceding Xephon /
Insight IS chapter.*

~~~~~

When writers learn of new publications and websites, they shouldn't hesitate to contact these firms and offer their services. Initially, these firms often rely on in-house writers or their own editors to provide content, and haven't yet placed ads seeking freelancers. Get your foot in the door early, like Murdoch did with this *IBM developer website*. (However, never hesitate to turn a new publication down if they don't pay!)

Since his first contact with this firm, Murdoch has written several articles for the *IBM developer website*, initially for a trial European version and following an approach by that section editor (the addressee of the emails below), for the central, US-based site.

Below are two emails that led to this high-paying assignment. Murdoch learned about the new site IBM was launching and sent an introductory email to the editor, offering to write for it. He says, "I sent the first email and duly received commissions for articles around suggestions 1, 6 and 8. She then asked me to elaborate on the cryptography suggestion (item 6) and this I did in detail in the second email. The result was an agreement to write a large article, split into seven sections (the six listed plus a seventh on resources). These brought in a total payment of £9,300.00, or approximately $15,000."

The articles were published beginning later that year and continued over the following year. They are currently online at the following URLs:

http://www-106.ibm.com/developerworks/security/library/s-crypt01.html?dwzone=security

http://www-106.ibm.com/developerworks/security/library/s-crypt02.html?dwzone=security

http://www-106.ibm.com/developerworks/security/library/s-crypt03.html?dwzone=security

What makes Murdoch's query a hit:
1. Initially offers not one, but two features in a hurry to help with the editor's launch.
2. Offers eight detailed yet brief article ideas (six are only one paragraph, yet provide ample detail), greatly increasing his chances of at least one sale.

The query and follow-up correspondence below were sent by email only after Murdoch sent an initial introductory email. Murdoch was paid $15,000 for his series of articles.

Murdoch's $15,000 Query

Hi [Editor's First Name],

Here are a few preliminary suggestions for features for the EU developerWorks site. You mentioned that the launch was in a week or so and with that in mind I could get a feature on the first item (SOAP) in on time. I'm going to Palm Springs on Saturday the 10th so that makes this week shorter and busier than might otherwise be the case, but it might be possible also to do a second one, such as the XML overview (3), for the launch.

1. Simple Object Access Protocol
(SOAP) is a protocol whereby XML data can invoke objects, and hence processes, remotely across the Web and without running into problems with firewalls. The group promoting the protocol to W3C for recognition as a standard includes both Microsoft and IBM (specifically Lotus) but not Oracle or Sun. I could tackle this in two separate ways (possibly do two articles, one on each). One approach would be to take a general overview looking broadly at what SOAP is and what it offers and where it fits in with other initiatives (I'm thinking here of matters such as BizTalk, ebXML and InfoGlide's Similarity Engine). A second approach would be to focus much more on technical issues and to look at the protocol in some detail. However, I certainly wouldn't be able to tackle this latter in this coming week so that would need to be a later submission, if of interest at all.

2. XML schemas and languages overview
As you'll know, there's been a steady development of schemas, typically for particular vertical industries. The main players here are the BizTalk Consortium, OASIS and, to some extent, OMG, UN/CEFACT and W3C. There are also specialist bodies such as RosettaNet and CommerceNet among others. I'm not sure how

many schemas have been published (but there are something like 140 on the BizTalk site) or how many recognised and relatively widely used XML languages exist (perhaps a couple of hundred depending on what criteria of use is employed). A fairly general feature looking at the arguments for schema and particular language development, what's involved, who's involved and why it matters (or doesn't!) might be of interest to bring developers up to date.

3. XML overview
There may be a place for a relatively short article on what XML is anyway and why it matters. I realise that sort of material is fairly easy to come by over the Web and in printed publications but it might still be appropriate for completeness as the site is launched. I'm thinking here of some of the technical issues, explanations of things like DTDs, schemas and so on, and what developments are taking place in presentation (CSSs and XSL) and in related matters to extend XML.

4. Oracle and XML
I mentioned when we spoke that Oracle is heavily committed to XML (as, of course, are IBM, Sun and Microsoft). XML is used extensively within Oracle 8i and is an important component of their just-released (finally) Internet File System (iFS). I could write a feature looking at this, commenting on the opportunities for developers as appropriate.

5. San Francisco project
This is something I'm aware of and have been tracking in a fairly general way for some time. That's to say, I understand its relevance and aims and with some additional research would be able to develop an appropriate article setting out in more detail what's involved.

6. Cryptography and cryptographic techniques

I've written several in-depth articles on different aspects of cryptography and I'd be interested in submitting one for this site. Although cryptographic techniques are of considerable, and growing, importance to eBusiness many developers seem not to understand much of the detail. It could therefore be useful to offer a feature covering the background in reasonable depth looking at, say:

> Symmetric encryption, specifically block ciphers, stream ciphers, hash codes and message authentication, with a number of instances such as DES, IDEA, Blowfish, etc.

> Asymetric (public key) encryption with instances such as RSA, Diffie-Hellman, etc.

> Advantages, disadvantages and vulnerabilities of various methods

> Practical deployment, typically using envelope mechanisms; PGP; digital signing and timestamping; certificates; SSL, S-HTTP, etc., etc., etc.

The major problem here is that the subject is very large and could easily run to well over reasonable limits for article size. However, assuming the general idea is of interest, I could tackle it by splitting it into a number of smaller articles dealing with particular sub-topics.

7. Profiling

There's a substantial growth in the area of profiling Web visitors and, at least in the more alert companies, linking this in to methods of monitoring and tracking customer information throughout the enterprise (I'm reluctant to use the somewhat jaded term CRM but, I guess, that's one way of putting it). There are several different techniques developing and being refined and which can often be used well together and according to different circumstance. I'm not suggesting here a technically detailed article (which would certainly not be practical for the whole subject area anyway) but one looking at what's happening so that developers can keep up to date and make judgments about what areas might usefully be followed up. The event I'm going to in Palm Springs is the user conference of ATG (Art Technology Group) one of the major players in this area albeit using only certain kinds of technology to track, monitor and personalise. It may well be that some interesting matter will come out of that which I could follow up with you later.

8. Components and CBD
You initially contacted me on account of the article I'd written on CBD for App Dev Advisor. I've also written other features for them, for Component Strategies and for others and I could certainly write on aspects of CBD if that were also an area of interest to you.

Apologies if this is a little sketchy but I wanted to get some ideas to you quickly, partly on account of your coming launch, partly as I'm to be away as I mentioned. If you'd like me to go ahead on any of these suggested articles then I'll be glad to do so. However, if you do want one or two for your launch then please let me know by return so that I can plan the week accordingly. I'll be in during Monday if you want to call to discuss things further and I'll be around some of the time on Tuesday but I expect to be out for most of the morning and during the latter part of the afternoon.

Thanks for sending the information on the IBM Technical Developer conference, which certainly sounds interesting. I'll follow up on that shortly.

Regards
Murdoch

Mudoch's Follow-up

Hi [Editor's First Name],

I promised earlier to get back to you with suggestions for some articles on relevant aspects of cryptography of interest to developers.

My feeling is that the subject is a coherent whole but because of the scope, it can reasonably be broken into sections, each of them self contained by also linking naturally to others. Perhaps the following divisions would be appropriate.

1. Introduction
This would be a fairly introductory look at the subject overall explaining the fundamental differences between the very long established category of secret key (symmetric) cryptography and the relatively new approach of public key (asymmetric) cryptography and touch on examples of each but without going into detail. It would also be relevant to touch on hash functions and message authentication codes, to consider the advantages and disadvantages of the two main categories of cryptography and to look at the practical applications of each including in such composite programs as PGP. The aim would be to give a developer unfamiliar with the subject some idea of the scope and what's involved.

2. Symmetric cryptography
Not all the algorithms are published and of those that are some are subject to royalty payments. However, this feature could look in more detail at aspects of secret key cryptography as currently used considering specifically the technicalities of block ciphers (DES, IDEA, Blowfish, etc.), stream ciphers, and other appropriate methods.

3. Asymmetric cryptography
As with 2., this would be a more detailed look at the techniques used, the advantages and disadvantages peculiar to this category and at how a developer should go about implementing existing algorithms into applications.

4. Practical applications
This feature could be something of a drawing together of different elements but also including a more detailed and practical study of some aspects such as hash functions, message authentication codes and digests, digital certificates and levels of signing authority, time stamping and digital signing and how to use appropriate elements.

5. Internet implications
Related to the above is the area of online use with a look at what's involved in S/MIME, SSL, S-HTTP and other methods. PGP and other hybrid systems could fit in here or perhaps in 4.

6. Practical implications
Implications as opposed to application, being the business of where other developing technologies fit in, most particularly smart cards and biometric methods of authentication. There's also the issue of local password protection and management and how developers might facilitate this in their applications. It might be better, of course, to bring that sort of material in to earlier features, most particularly under 4. or 5. but I feel it could equally stand on its own. It's partly a question of how far to go as there are related matters such as single sign-on, the use of PDA or laptops and matters of that sort, which are relevant but perhaps somewhat peripheral to the thrust of a site aimed at developers.

Let me know what you think, if you would. I can always look further at some of these if you want.

Regards
Murdoch

National Public Radio: All Things Considered - $2,000

Bruce Farr is an Arizona-based freelance writer and editor. In addition to his ongoing work as a Commentator for National Public Radio's nationally broadcast program "All Things Considered", Bruce has published numerous articles in a wide range of genres, including business, travel, humor, and healthcare. He is currently working on a book-length collection of his own essays. Bruce lives in Scottsdale, Arizona with his wife, Sharon Combes-Farr, and daughter, Erin.

~~~~~

Last year, Bruce Farr, a marketing manager, was part of a mass layoff at the company he had worked at for several years. He said, "When the dust settled, I thought I would spend a while trying to get back into writing, which I had done as a freelancer for years, most recently in the mid-90s. Among other queries I sent out, I put together a proposal regarding the experience of being laid off at the exact same age my dad was when he lost his longtime job many years ago. I sent it off to National Public Radio's program *All Things Considered*. (Their *Commentaries* are a mainstay of the nationally broadcast program.) The next day, I received a call from their *Commentaries* editor, telling me she was very interested in using the piece."

Perhaps the most important key to Bruce's query and subsequent sale is that he tied his personal experiences to current events (the economy), instantly making his story "news". Being able to tie any article idea to current events greatly increases your chance of a sale!

After some minor editing to bring the piece into a more "radio-friendly" format, Bruce went to his local NPR affiliate and taped the story for airing. When it ran last December, the response was overwhelming. People from across the country were calling NPR, trying to get in touch with Bruce.

Bruce adds, "Some of them just offered support, but others actually offered me help finding a job! One of the callers was a VP from a Biotech company in Tucson. He asked if I could come down (from Phoenix) and talk to him about my background. I did so, and ended up with a 4-month contract that paid me handsomely! Frankly, although I've been a 'marketing person' for many years, it had never occurred to me to use my writing ability as a channel to market myself."

What makes Bruce's query a hit:
1. Good hook. The first sentence immediately draws the reader into the story.
2. Portrays his father with warmth and humor, making the reader identify with him and his father on a personal level.
3. Links father's old experience to his own current situation (coincidence stories are always intriguing).
4. Ties both stories to current events (the struggling economy).

The query below was submitted according to NPR's online submission guidelines. You can find these, along with a list of their shows, at: http://www.npr.org/about/pitch. NPR paid Bruce $2,000 for his story.

Bruce's $2,000 Query

Editor's Full Name, Commentaries Editor
National Public Radio
Washington, DC

Dear [Editor]:

In 1976, when he was 52 years old, my father was laid off. The textile factory where he had worked for 35 years as a loom fixer had struggled and been bought out. Its new owners consolidated what was left of any value and moved it down south where labor and materials could be gotten much cheaper. He looked for work for months, but, finally, with the bills and worries piling up, he took a low-paying job as a janitor at the state university where I was then a student.

Almost daily, as I sat between classes drinking coffee with my college pals, I'd see my father across the rows of noisy tables in the Student Union, pushing a laundry cart piled high with dirty sheets and towels. We'd catch each other's eye and smile and wave, and sometimes he'd even join us on his break and share a couple of his famously lame jokes. But what my buddies couldn't begin to guess was that the sight of him in this state filled me with an awful mixture of pity and revulsion. They never sensed the invisible badge of shame we both wore about the circumstances that had befallen him.

So it seemed more than ironic when, a few weeks ago, at 52, I was let go from my job as a marketing manager at company where I had worked for several years. Although separated by the distance of more than 20 years, the worry and pain I had felt vicariously through my father was suddenly my own, and the uncertainty of what to do next loomed very large indeed.

I would like to propose a Commentary for *All Things Considered* that describes, in greater depth, the mixture of emotions and eventual actions these oddly coincidental events triggered. In times of considerable economic uncertainty, the impact of job loss on individuals and their families can be far-reaching and critically important to explore. It is a story I think your listeners would benefit from hearing.

I thank you for your consideration, and look forward to hearing from you.

Sincerely,

Bruce Farr

SmartMoney - $5,000

Susie Eley is a freelance writer in New York City. Her work has been published in Parents Magazine, Time Out New York, and others and she has been editor of Golden Falcon, Dance Teacher, and Dance Spirit magazines.

~~~~~

Susie Eley found some unexpected free time earlier this year and wrote a story about her husband's adventure race experience for fun. She said, "I passed it on to a colleague who had a friend at *SmartMoney*, with whom she once worked with at *Forbes*. You know the drill...it's often the contact who helps you get a foot in the door."

As Susie knows, writers should never hesitate to ask their contacts in the industry to suggest other editors who might like their work. Just dropping a name may be all you need to get your query read, and not stuffed in the slush pile.

With the contact name and her professional query below, Susie ended up with the most profitable assignment she's ever received. She adds, "Funny, I really thought nobody would ever buy this piece, and it turned out to be my most lucrative work in over 10 years of editing and writing."

While *SmartMoney* is a financial magazine, they also publish human-interest stories that address issues of finding balance in life (career, family, health, etc.). Around the time Susie's article was published, the *New York Times* ran an article about how finance magazines are attracting new readers by broadening their editorial to include more lifestyle / human interest stories. *SmartMoney* was used as an example in the article.

What makes Susie's query a hit:
1. Drops a name (uses name of mutual acquaintance to get her foot in the door).
2. Has already made plans to obtain professional photographs.
3. Includes brief yet impressive list of credits.

This query was sent via email. *SmartMoney* paid Susie $5,000 for her article.

Susie's $5,000 Query

Dear Mr. [Editor's Last Name],

[Editor's Colleague's Name] recommended that I send you the attached article about a 24-hour adventure race that my husband, John, and two teammates participated in several months ago. The 85-mile race, which began at Harriman State Park in upstate New York and finished at Chelsea Piers, took John's team nearly 18½ hours to finish. The race required a grueling mix of running in the woods without a path, mountain biking, in-line skating, swimming, and the piece de resistance, rappelling down the starboard side of the U.S.S. Intrepid.

The public relations agency has photographs from every leg of the race--from kayaking down the Hudson River, to running across the George Washington Bridge. The photos are high resolution and readily available for publication.

I'm a freelance writer and a part-time editor at *Promenade* magazine in New York City. I have held senior editorial positions at *Golden Falcon*, a travel publication in the Persian Gulf, *Dance Teacher* and *Dance Spirit* magazines in New York. I have written over 100 articles for these magazines, as well as for *Parents, Time Out New York, Jewish Woman* and others.

I hope you will consider this story for publication in *SmartMoney*. I can be reached via e-mail or by phone at xxx-xxx-xxxx.

Sincerely,

Susan Eley

Unique Opportunities: The Physician's Resource - $2,500

Marcia Layton Turner, a best-selling author known for her business and marketing books, had trouble breaking into writing for national magazines. Her first queries just didn't seem to be hitting the mark. After reading up on the subject of queries and researching target markets, she tried again with an evergreen pitch regarding marketing for retailers. It was successful and started Marcia on the road to regular article assignments. That was two years ago. She now derives nearly 50% of her income from magazine assignments.

Some of Marcia's books include Kmart's Ten Deadly Sins: How incompetence tainted an American Icon (Wiley, 2003), The Complete Idiot's Guide to Starting a Small Business (Macmillan, 1998), and Successful Fine Art Marketing (Consultant Press, 1993). Publications she has written for include ePregnancy, REALTOR, Florida Realtor, Specialty Retail Report, New Age Retailer, Country Business, Progressive Rentals, American Painting Contractor, New England Bride, and Beauty Store Business. You can reach Marcia via her website at: http://www.marcialaytonturner.com

~~~~~

Marcia Layton Turner received an assignment from *Unique Opportunities* via phone last fall for a 3,000-word article that paid $0.75 per word for First North American Print Rights, with unlimited use on their website (which, she says, was fine since she didn't intend to sell it elsewhere).

Although Marcia had never heard of *Unique Opportunities* before finding it in a recent edition of Writer's Market, a trade magazine paying $0.75 per word was one she definitely wanted to write for.

She adds, "It took a few months before I came up with a topic that I thought would fit their editorial slant, which I researched at their website. That single email, with no follow-up, was what landed the job. I always prefer to pitch via email since the responses tend to come faster. The job ended up being very painless, the editor was a joy to work with, and payment came very swiftly."

What makes Marcia's query a hit:
1. Good hook. Gets right to the heart of the topic without a boring introduction.
2. Nice human-interest angle for a trade publication.
3. Great last paragraph; enthusiastic but not pushy.

This query was sent via email. *Unique Opportunities* paid Marcia $2,500 for her article.

Marcia's $2,500 Query

Dear Ms. [Editor's Last Name],

How can young physicians get established in a new community when they don't have a network of friends and family to turn to? For most new physicians, moving to a new community means starting over, meeting new colleagues, and making new friends. Increasingly, however, medical professional organizations are recognizing the challenges that physicians new to the community face and are creating new sections specifically geared to helping them get established and feel welcome.

I'd like to write an article for Unique Opportunities titled "Making New Connections" that provides information on these new young physician networking groups, incorporating interviews with physicians who joined and have benefited from their association with such groups. I envision the article as a 1,500-word piece that details how to find such a group, and how to make the most of membership.

I am a professional freelancer and award-winning author who has penned more than ten business books, including The Unofficial Guide to Starting a Small Business and How to Think Like the World's Greatest Marketing Minds, and countless business and trade articles. Some of my recent clips include Business 2.0, Office.com, Seed World, and Flowers & Profits; I've attached a couple here for your review.

I'd love the chance to write this article for Unique Opportunities and welcome your feedback on this topic.

Best regards,

Marcia

A lifestyle magazine - $2,200 for the article; $50,000 for the subsequent book

Mark Henricks has worked full-time as a freelance journalist since 1987, and has written nearly 2,000 articles on business, personal finance, technology, books, sports, health, travel, and other topics for more than 100 publications including American Way, Boys' Life, CNET, Entrepreneur, National Geographic Kids, The New York Times, PCWorld, Southwest Spirit, StartupJournal, and The Wall Street Journal. He has also authored, co-authored, or ghostwritten 11 non-fiction books, is currently working with a collaborator on a book about values and ethics at home and work, and has appeared on NPR Marketplace radio as a commentator on lifestyle business.

~~~~~

Two years ago, Mark Henricks wrote a query letter for an article on entrepreneurs that resulted in a $2,000 assignment from a lifestyle magazine for first serial rights. After reading this, you'll understand why we can't divulge the name of the magazine. The article was later posted to the magazine's website, which resulted in an additional $200 payment for electronic rights, making the total earned from the article $2,200. Mark had been working for the magazine for a couple of years as a freelance columnist, writing their business book reviews and contributing occasional features, when he proposed this article to one of the editors using the query featured below.

Mark adds, "There's more. I pitched the article with the hope that the resulting assignment would pay me to research a book proposal on the topic. I'd already sent 40 or so query letters pitching the book to publishers and received seven expressions of interest. I used those letters to interest an agent, who eventually got a $50,000 advance on the proposal. The sample chapter in the proposal was largely the lifestyle magazine's article, rewritten and expanded. The book was published last August in hardcover as *Not Just a Living: The Complete Guide to Creating a Business that Gives You a Life* (Perseus). The paperback edition was also recently released."

Mark's query letter has a strong human-interest slant (who wouldn't want to do what these people do for a living?), and mentions statistics from Dun and Bradstreet, which validate his claims. Many writers find and use statistics, not only to convince editors of the validity of their statements, but also to come up with ideas for queries themselves!

What makes Mark's query a hit:
1. Good hook.
2. Great human-interest angle; makes the reader wish they were one of those people!
3. Statistics validate statements and show Mark has done his research.

Mark was paid $2,200 for his article, and earned a $50,000 advance for the subsequent book.

Mark's $2,200+ Query

[Editor's First Name]:

Four million of the nation's 20 million small business owners aren't in it for the money. They're in it for the lifestyle. These Lifestyle Entrepreneurs are clustered in appealing fields that sound more like hobbies than businesses, from bookstore owner and fishing guide to dog trainer and ski school operator. All have one thing in common: They start and run businesses because owning their own company improves their lives by giving them more free time, more money for hours worked or greater opportunities to have fun--not because they hope to rule a commercial empire.

Sacrilege? Not to 21 percent of 2,000 small business owners Dun & Bradstreet surveyed last year. These Optimizers, as D&B dubbed them, are the second largest of five entrepreneurial groups identified. Compared to the rest, they were far more into personal rewards of entrepreneurship, focusing on freedom, flexibility and fun rather than economic expansion. Surprisingly, this large and distinctive group receives short shrift from most entrepreneurship experts and observers, who focus on tips increasing sales, adding employees and expanding businesses, often at great personal cost to the lifestyles of the entrepreneurs who lead them.

[Name of article] will look at the trend toward starting a business that is more about giving you a life than making you a mogul. Along with stats and explanations from experts, I'll include interviews with entrepreneurs who have begun businesses primarily in order to address lifestyle needs.

Thanks for your interest. Is it a go?

Best,

Mark Henricks

Worth's 'Giving e-Magazine' - $2,000

Nancy Gates is a freelance writer in central Pennsylvania. She "cut her teeth" as a newspaper reporter covering everything from 12-alarm fires to game wardens on patrol. She has contributed features to numerous publications, including Central PA Magazine, Mystery Scene, American Profile, and Simple Livin.'

~~~~~

Nancy Gates wrote what she thought was a "mighty tempting query" about legendary college football coach Jerry Sandusky, who is also the founder of The Second Mile, a community outreach program based in State College, Pennsylvania. She sent the query to *Reader's Digest* feeling quite confident. She said, "I knew I had just pitched a can't-miss story!"

Unfortunately, *Reader's Digest* never responded. So, she sent the query to a few more magazines. They didn't respond, either.

A few months later, Nancy found an ad at a freelance writer's site for *Giving*, a startup ezine devoted to philanthropy, produced by *Worth Magazine*. The ad requested profiles of famous and not-so-famous activists who used their wealth and status to promote worthy endeavors of all kinds. The ad stressed that the editors didn't want profiles of celebrities with fat wallets who just toss cash to their favorite charities; the profile subjects were to be true philanthropists with total devotion to their various causes. The pay for an accepted article was to be $1.50 per word.

The editor was looking for immediate material, so Nancy opened the file containing her Sandusky query (the one previously sent to *Reader's Digest*), copied and pasted it into an e-mail, then simply deleted the one specific reference to *Reader's Digest*. The subject matter was so perfect for *Giving* that no further changes were necessary.

Within an hour of sending out the query by email, the editor of *Giving* emailed Nancy Gates saying the profile of Sandusky would be perfect for his publication. He then requested some of her clips. Nancy happily and instantly sent those to him via email as well. Another hour passed, and the editor emailed her back again. asking her to phone him. When she called, he asked a few more questions, and she shared some inspiring anecdotes, illustrating Sandusky's boundless devotion to children.

Nancy said, "I held my breath and then the editor gave me the assignment for 800 words, at $1.50 per word, and said the contract would be on its way!"

After signing the contract and beginning the researching and interviewing process, Nancy called the editor again and offered to do a substantial sidebar piece focusing on the interaction between some of the Second Mile teens and their mentors. He liked that idea, too, so her total word count (and pay) went up.

Nancy adds, "Then, as we were talking, the editor paused and said it seemed that I'd done a lot of work for this article, like making two 90-mile roundtrips for interviews. (*Worth* did reimburse me for mileage.) He asked if I felt I was entitled to a slightly higher pay rate. After I regained consciousness, I said, 'Mmmm, yes, I think that's fair.' So, at a word count of about 1,300, I wound up earning $2,000. Let me just note that I never thought an editor would ever ask me, 'Do you think we should pay you a little more?' That was truly a once-in-a-lifetime moment."

Unfortunately, before the story was published, *Worth* elected to terminate *Giving e-magazine*. Nancy was paid, but her story was never published. She was deeply disappointed because the topic was very important to her and is one she feels people should know about.

She said, "I would have attempted to place the article and sidebar in another publication but, in exchange for that great paycheck, I gave up all my rights to the material, which is lesson in itself for freelancers! It's hard to accept that a story you love won't ever see the light of day because you didn't retain any rights. Had I only known that *Giving's* lifespan would be so brief, I would have bartered for less money in exchange for First North American Rights only."

Many writers who sell all rights now request a clause in their contracts requesting rights be returned to them if a publication fails to publish the piece within a specific period of time, or if the publication goes out of business. The writer, of course, is permitted to keep the payment because none of the factors that resulted in non-publication were the writer's fault.

And what about those publications that seem to hold an article hostage after they've purchased first rights only? A writer can't sell second or reprint rights to another editor until the first buyer has published the piece. If it's never published, it's in limbo, and the writer is contractually banned from pursuing more income for that piece while it's in limbo...even if it remains there forever.

Writers selling first rights should always include a clause in their contracts stating the publication's "first rights" will automatically revert to second, reprint, or one-time rights should the publication fail to publish the article within a specific time-frame, and that the writer is then free to sell first or other rights to another publication. And, of course, the writer would also keep the payment in these circumstances because the late or non-publication was due to the publication's actions, not the writer's.

You may be wondering why Nancy didn't ask *Worth* to return the rights to her for this article. Companies that publish numerous magazines can occasionally find a place for purchased, yet unpublished articles. If they can't, they can usually find another publication willing to buy those articles. So, asking a company that owns numerous publications for the rights back to your story (without returning the money) might work, but usually does not.

What makes Nancy's query a hit:
1. Mentions celebrity in first sentence.
2. Well-written; looks like an article, not a query letter.
3. Is brief, but provides lots of information; it's obvious Nancy has already researched and is familiar with the topic.
4. Passion for the topic is evident in the query and portrays warmth in Nancy's writing.

This query was sent via email. Nancy earned $2,000 for her article.

Nancy's $2,000 Query

Dear [Editor's Name]:

In football-crazed central Pennsylvania, Jerry Sandusky, defensive coordinator for Penn State's Nittany Lions, has become a familiar, and beloved, figure.

But Sandusky's local hero status stems from much more than his gift for X's and O's. Besides helping to make the Lions a perennial powerhouse in college football, Sandusky is the founder of the Second Mile, a rapidly growing volunteer organization that provides moral and academic guidance to youths across Pennsylvania.

Thanks to hundreds of community volunteers, the Second Mile offers the Friendship Program, which coaches kids on building and maintaining healthy relationships; the Peak Program, which provides mentoring, and the Nittany Lion Tip Cards Program: sports cards that feature advice on coping with life's dilemmas and challenges, hand-delivered to youngsters by Nittany Lions players. The Second Mile also conducts an annual three-day Challenge Camp, emphasizing teamwork, goal-setting, and academic achievement.

A past recipient of the NAACP's Human Rights Award, Sandusky is also the author of the classic coaching manual, "Developing Linebackers The Penn State Way," proceeds of which help fund the Second Mile. Sandusky, age 55, is enjoying his final campaign with the Lions, and will retire after the current season in order to devote his complete attention to the burgeoning Second Mile program, which now serves 150,000 youngsters statewide.

I would welcome the opportunity to profile philanthropist and coach Jerry Sandusky for your new e-zine, "Giving."

I am a freelance journalist and my credits include Central PA Magazine, The Cleveland Plain Dealer, and The Lutheran, among other publications.

Thank you for your consideration.

Sincerely,
Nancy Gates

Bio-IT World - $2,500 (CDN)

Sherene Chen-See launched her freelance writing career two years ago. Her journalism background encompasses a wide variety of genres, focusing mostly on medicine, science, and educational articles for pre-teens. She also specializes in corporate writing for the pharmaceutical industry.

~~~~~

Bio-IT World is a trade magazine that focuses on the combination of medical and computer technology. Sherene Chen-See was enthusiastic about landing an assignment with them and carefully contemplated which topic to pitch. She read their magazine, contacted one of their editors to get a better idea of what they were looking for, searched the Internet extensively for a suitable topic, and then, finally, sat down to write the query letter. After a few follow-ups, they bought her story.

In the first sentence of her query letter, Sherene mentions the name of her previous phone contact at the magazine.

What makes Sherene's query a hit:
1. Drops a name.
2. Brief, yet contains numerous facts.
3. Presents both positive and negative aspects of the story, ensuring the story will be balanced.
4. Mentions privacy, an issue that has been in the news frequently (the story can be tied to current events).

The article length was 1250 words and included a diagram. Payment was $2,500 (CDN) on acceptance. All rights (print and electronic) were originally assigned to *Bio-IT World*. However, the magazine granted second rights for all media to the author six months after publication. This query was sent via email.

Sherene's $2,500 (CDN) Query

Mark Uehling recommended that I contact you with queries.

Imagine a system where all public health records are kept in one central database that can be accessed by health care providers across the country at any given time. Patients who see multiple physicians or have tests done at a variety of labs would have all relevant information zapped into their central file. Outbreaks could be identified and tracked sooner, thus enabling more effective public health action. This capability would increase efficiency and cost savings in the health care system and could prove invaluable to hospitals when immediate background on a patient is required. The Canadian Integrated Public Health Surveillance (CIPHS) project aims to do just this.

The CIPHS integrated computer database applications will enable front-line health workers and lab personnel to systematically collect and collate medical surveillance data using the Public Health Information System (PHIS) and Laboratory Data Management System (LDMS). PHIS is an automated, integrated system that allows access to one client record by many public health providers. The system supports public health provider interventions, tracking, case management, communicable disease surveillance, and sharing of immunization information. LDMS is a LIMS system that can hold relevant patient information related to lab tests and information on case investigations, and link this to a particular group of specimens.

I am a Canadian freelance writer who specializes in health/medical-related issues (résumé attached). I would like to write a 1,500-word feature on CIPHS, which would encompass the need, advantages and challenges that pertain to such a system. I would also be interested in finding out how the public's right to privacy of medical records would be affected by this system Kindly advise by September 30 whether you are interested Thanks.

A major New York financial services brokerage - $3,500

Janet C. Arrowood is the Managing Director of The Write Source, Inc. She is a full-time, freelance financial, insurance, legal, and accounting services writer, and has been writing for these industries since 1992. Her work has appeared in Advisor Today, Variable Products Specialist, The Colorado Lawyer, WestLaw's database, Financial Playbook, Financial Services Journal Online, InsuranceNewsletters.com, The Denver Business Journal, and other media. In addition, she is the author of three books: The Professional Advisor's Insurance Desk Reference (CLE in Colorado, Inc., 2000); Marketing for Results -- A Practical Toolkit for Small Businesses and Professional Advisors (Booklocker.com-http://www.booklocker.com/books/976.html); Living With Wildfires - Prevention, Preparation, and Recovery (Bradford Publishing - http://wildfires.bradfordpublishing.com); and a booklet about Long-term Care, Medicare, and Medicaid (Bradford Publishing, 2001).

Her current projects include more mini-magazines (see below), co-authoring a book about life and health insurance for pre-licensees, and an applied mathematics book for learners of English as a Second Language. Janet can be reached via her website at http://www.thewritesource.org, or via email at thewritesource@earthlink.net.

~~~~~

When Janet Arrowood realized she could not be all things to all people (the typical writer's approach), she decided to specialize, and subsequently landed several lucrative assignments as a financial / insurance writer.

Janet's query letter below is different from the others featured in this book. She doesn't pitch an article. She proposes the creation (writing and layout) of an entire "mini-magazine" to be published by the client, which is a financial services firm.

Janet said, "I landed the assignment by actively and regularly soliciting a number of the top financial advisor firms around the country, using their top management as sources for my articles in other national financial publications (for the FA industry, primarily) and sending copies of my draft articles to their managers and compliance staff for comments, correction, and review. This ensured that, when I went looking for paying assignments later the right people would know who I was and that I am knowledgeable and credible."

Janet adds, "The keys to freelancing success are obvious and ignored - specialize and focus and persist! Now I am a financial, insurance / business writer and the assignments are flowing nicely - regular gigs at an insurance newsletter, assignments for local papers, frequent magazine articles (assigned, not queried) for Advisor Today and Financial Playbook, audio tape programs (development and voice over) for the Certified Financial Advisor. and I think I just landed a $10,000 assignment (from a query) to co-author an insurance training manual (and there's lots of other work there as a financial services trainer)."

What makes Janet's proposal a hit:
1. Janet's website URL portrays a professional organization (not that of a single freelance writer); and note the professional title under her signature.
2. Unique idea designed to help the client earn more money (market their services); it's a win/win situation for the client and for Janet.
3. Extremely professional and nicely formatted (the format of the query would, of course, reflect on the design expectations for the mini-magazine).

4. Shows she is a successful writer with numerous published pieces by inviting the editor to simply search for her name in a search engine.

Janet's query was successful and she was able to hire other writers and layout personnel to help. The entire project budget was $12,000. Janet's profit was $3,500. The client retained all rights to the finished product.

Janet's $3,500 Proposal

The Write Source, Inc
Mailing Address
City, State, Zip
Phone xxx.xxx.xxxx
http://www.thewritesource.org

Manager's Name
Company Name
Mailing Address
City, State, Zip

Dear [Manager's Name],

Motivating your Financial Advisors (FAs) at any time is a challenge, but in a declining or stagnant market environment it is even harder. One technique I have found to be very successful is to leverage the energy and information from your annual conferences by providing both qualifiers and those who didn't make the cut with "proceedings"—a kind of "mini-magazine" highlighting the educational and motivational aspects of the "heavy hitter" conferences. In addition to serving as documentation of the educational aspects of the event (making the IRS happy), this "mini-magazine" will also capture the atmosphere, energy, and excitement of being around other top performers and top-level managers, experts, and analysts. While nothing can take the place of actually being there, the "mini-magazine" I am proposing comes close.

I propose the following services, products, and turnaround times:

- A 12-page magazine with a full-page ad from your firm on the back cover, internal artwork supplied by your firm, and several half-page ads (all delivered to me no later than the end of the conference). The magazine will consist of 10-12 300-400 word articles, several sidebars, and quotes from your top management, FAs, analysts, sales directors, and others as you specify.

- Three on-site writers to document events, presentations, comments, and speeches as they happen.

- A completed magazine, delivered electronically, two weeks after the close of the conference.

I am a full-time freelance financial services writer with over 12 years of direct financial and insurance services experience, including sales and FA management. I have done similar work for other major financial services companies and can supply copies upon request. In addition, much of my work is available online; the simplest way is to "google" my name, "Janet C. Arrowood" (in quotes) and then select the material you find most relevant. The other writers involved are also nationally known freelance financial writers.

I anticipate the cost for the above project to be $12,000 to deliver the complete magazine in electronic format, plus the expenses for the writers on assignment.

Thank-you for your time and consideration.

Sincerely,

Janet C. Arrowood
Managing Director

General Pitch Letters

Abbi's Form Letter - $30,000-$45,000 annually

Abbi Perets lives in sunny Southern California with her husband and their two daughters. She writes regularly about parenting, technology, health, and travel for major magazines and websites. She is currently co-authoring a book on back pain with her father. Check out more of Abbi's strategies for success online at: http://www.SuccessfulFreelanceWriting.com

~~~~~

When interviewing successful freelancers for this book, I was determined to find a successful writer who relies on a standard form letter to solicit work...a kind and generous writer who was willing to share their successful form letter with other writers. And I was blessed to find Abbi Perets!

Wouldn't it be nice to just fire off a form letter to publications that are seeking writers for assignments, or even those that have a stable of freelancers but aren't currently running any ads? Abbi's form letter below is so successful that she can choose her assignments. She, of course, pursues the highest-paying projects!

Abbi shares her secret for earning $30,000-$45,000 annually using this method: "Mine isn't quite a standard query letter -- it's not the tailored piece I occasionally send out to magazines. It's a standard form letter, really, that I send out by email all the time. It almost always gets a reply -- even if the reply is just, 'Thanks, we'll keep you on file.' And, often, the letter results in high-paying work. I only work four hours a day because my children are still small, so I look specifically for high-paying assignments I can handle in short chunks of time."

The assignments resulting from Abbi's form letter below bring in $30,000-$45,000 annually.

Abbi's Form Letter

Dear [Editor's Name]:

Do you ever outsource any of your writing?

I'm a freelance writer with a decade of professional experience. I've been published in many print and online magazines: NBCi.com, Myria.com, PlanetExpat.com, and other highly-publicized Web sites, Travelocity, Pregnancy, International Living, and other newsstand magazines. I'm a frequent contributor to Tech Republic. I write and ghostwrite regularly for a high tech trade publication, Diversity/Careers in Engineering and Information Technology, and I'm a senior contributing editor with ePregnancy Magazine. I also served as contributing author for two books published by McGraw-Hill, Ace the IT Résumé and Ace the IT Interview.

Before going freelance, I lived in Israel and worked for the leading export marcom company in Tel Aviv. I copywrote thousands of pages for high tech companies including ECI Telecom, Elbit Systems, Edusoft, and Orange. In addition, I was the senior editor for the largest project the company had ever launched, Africana.com, a portal for the African and African American communities that was backed by a joint venture of Microsoft and Encarta. Stateside, I've written marketing collateral for dozens of diverse corporations that create everything from semiconductors to innovative programs for managing Hepatitis.

You can visit my Web site, http://www.DearAbbi.com, where my résumé and many clips are posted.

If you need a writer -- for occasional or ongoing assignments --
please contact me.

Sincerely,
Abbi Perets

Large telecom firm - $3,000

David Geer is a full-time freelance writer and owner of Gee *Communications. David specializes in technical, business, and* *general writing and journalism as well as corporate writing* *MarCom, and Web writing. His clips and credits span 130 projects* *for 30 clients and publications including The Engineering News* *Record, IEEE's Computer magazine, Arnold IT, and Accurate* *Information, Inc. You can contact David through his website at* *http://www.geercom.com*

~~~~~

David Geer is a tireless self-marketer. He has written numerous articles for my publications (*WritersWeekly.com* and *The Write* *Markets Report*) and, while some of his queries aren't quite right for our needs, I am always willing to work with him. If one of his ideas isn't quite what I'm looking for, I'll often suggest a different angle.

For example, recently David queried me with an article idea on how to teach writers how to be more editor-friendly, thus increasing the possibility of regular assignments. Since I am an advocate for writers' rights, and my opinion is that editors should be more writer-friendly (not the other way around), I asked for David to put a different twist on his idea. My ideas included telling editors they should answer writers' emails faster, treat writers with more respect (and a smile!), be happy to intervene when their accounting department fails to pay a writer on time, and more. Almost as fast as my finger clicked send, David fired back an email not only agreeing with me, but also adding a list of his own ideas on how editors can be more writer-friendly. I, of course, ordered that article! And, it was very popular with our readers!

David has a personable, upbeat personality and can easily make any editor feel like his friend. His flexibility and endless stream of ideas (he sends me new queries often but is never pushy) make him hard to turn down. These traits are what have made David a successful freelancer.

The pitch letter below, sent to a large telecom firm (that we are not permitted to name), brought in $3,000. The simple email pitch was in response to an advertisement David found online for a firm seeking writers with specific telecom writing experience. David did not waste the editor's time by sending more than they asked for. They wanted experienced writers for assignments and his résumé proves his eligibility. Note the formatting of and information provided in his email résumé (lots of writers ask us about how to create a writer's résumé!).

Also, note that David publishes his clips at his website for easy access by editors. This enables him to provide clips without sending email attachments. Editors typically do not like email attachments because of virus fears.

What makes David's pitch a hit:
1. Doesn't send more than the editor requested in the ad.
2. Offers résumé in clean email format.
3. No attachments; offers links to clips on his website.

This pitch was sent via email. The telecom firm paid David $3,000 for the resulting assignment.

David's $3,000 Pitch

From: David Geer
Sent: Monday, December 10
Subject: freelance opportunity

[Editor's First Name],

Résumé below. Clips are at: http://www.geercom.com/clips.html

David Geer
Street Address   *Primary Phone: xxx-xxx-xxxx*
City, State, Zip   *Fax: xxx-xxx-xxxx*
URL: *http://geercom.com*   *d@geercom.com*

Freelance Journalist, Writer

TARGET JOB
Desired Job Type: Temporary/Contract/Project

Site Location: Off-Site

Summary:

I am a full-time freelance journalist and writer. I have specialties in technology, computers, wireless, PR writing, music, fitness, psychology, how to and general interest. I am available by contract. I telecommute.

EXPERIENCE   9/2001-Present   Wireless Business &

	Technology, Montvale, NJ Writer *Write features by contract.*
9/2001-10/2001	Geek.com, Boston, MA Columnist *Wrote two column articles.*
8/2001	eReleases (PR Fuel Newsletter), Baltimore, MD Writer *Wrote newsletter articles.*
8/2001-Present	Open Directory Project - N/A Category Editor, Journalist
7/2001-Present	Computer Buyer's Guide & Handbook, NY, NY Writer *Write features by contract.*
6/2001-10/2001	Smart Computing, Lincoln, NE Writer *Wrote features by contract.*
6/2001-Present	Webseed, Cody, WY Writer *Softwaresupportsite.com* *Writer*
1/2001-6/2001	Hostingtech Magazine, Alexandria, VA Contributor *Wrote two features.*
11/2000	Briefme, NY, NY

Classical & Opera e-zine.
Contributing Music Editor

7/2000-4/2001   PageWise, Austin, TX
Author
Wrote 69 articles.

1/1998-7/1999   Songwriter's Monthly,
Philadelphia, PA
Contributing Freelance
Writer
Wrote two articles.

EDUCATION 5/1993   Lake Erie College
US-OH-Painesville
Bachelor's Degree
Bachelor of Arts in
Psychology
3.4 Cum. GPA.

Best Regards,
David Geer
d@geercom.com
http://geercom.com
WAP site: tagtag.com/geercom
Mail to: Street Address
City, State, Zip
Phone: xxx-xxx-xxxx
eFax: xxx-xxx-xxxx

ThirdAge.com - $2,000

Linda Tagliaferro is a freelance writer based in a suburb of New York City. She has written for national publications including The New York Times, and Maxim, and she's the author of 21 books ranging from The Complete Idiot's Guide to Decoding Your Genes, and an A&E Biography Book on Bruce Lee, to alphabet books for children. She can be reached via email at: Linda5997@aol.com

~~~~~

Linda Tagliaferro begins her pitch by boldly stating her mission. She wants to write for *Thirdage.com*. She then quickly mentions her qualifications, which are quite impressive (she's a regular contributor to the New York Times). In additional, Linda offers transparencies to accompany her work. This implies she is also a professional photographer, which will save the editor time on jobs that require photographs.

When an editor needs an article in a hurry, they run through their list of known writers in their heads. Who would be willing to help them out in an emergency? Who can deliver? Linda's final paragraph offers herself as that writer. It's a great addition to this pitch!

What makes Linda's pitch a hit:
1. Short, targeted, and honest.
2. Mentions impressive job title.
3. Offers transparencies to accompany assignments.
4. Offers herself as a "seasoned writer who can work on a tight deadline."

The pitch below was sent via email. It resulted in a $2,000 assignment from *ThirdAge.com.*

Linda's $2,000 Pitch

Dear ThirdAgers,

I'd like to write for thirdage.com. I've been a professional writer for 10 years, which includes 5 years as a regular contributor for The New York Times. My articles have also appeared in national publications that run the gamut from Boy's Life to Modern Maturity. I can also provide high-quality color transparencies of my work to accompany articles. Enclosed please find 3 clips.

In addition to my magazine and newspaper work, I'm also the author of 5 books, including The Complete Idiot's Guide to Decoding Your Genes (in Macmillan's popular Complete Idiot's series) and Bruce Lee (an A&E Biography Book for Young Adults.)

My greatest expertise is in travel and parenting issues. I've written for Big Apple Parent, a New York City publication, for 8 years, and covered issues from home schooling to family travel for them. I've traveled to most of the countries in Europe, most of the islands in the Caribbean, as well as parts of Africa and South America. Denmark was my home for 6 1/2 years, Italy for 6 months and Indonesia for 7 months.

Please give me a call if you need a seasoned writer who can work on a tight deadline. I look forward to hearing from you.

Sincerely,
Linda Tagliaferro

P.S. Please keep the clips.

Linda Tagliaferro
Mailing Address

City, State, Zip
Phone Number
Email Address

Natural Remedies – $11,300+

Meredith Gould has written extensively for popular, professional, and trade audiences. Her books and magazine articles focus on lifestyle, health, recovery, and practical spirituality. She is the author of four books: Deliberate Acts of Kindness: Service as a Spiritual Practice (Doubleday, 2002); Working at Home: Making it Work for You (Storey, 2000); and Staying Sober: Tips for Working a Twelve Step Program of Recovery (Hazelden, 1999). The Catholic Home: Celebrations and Traditions for Holidays, Feast Days, and Every Day, due out from Doubleday next year, received an imprimatur from the Catholic Church.

Her articles and essays have appeared in a wide range of publications including: American Health, Changes, Clarity, Nation's Business, National Business Employment Weekly, Natural Health, New Age Journal, New Woman, Utne Reader (reprinted twice!), and Vegetarian Times. She also reviews books for the Times of Trenton.

A freelancer since 1989, Meredith has provided marketing communications advice and editorial services to a range of corporate and nonprofit clients. She coaches a select number of individual writers each year and gives public talks about freelancing and book publishing. You can learn more about Meredith at: http://www.meredithgould.com

~~~~~

In 1997, Meredith Gould answered a New York Times classified ad, appearing under the "editorial" section, which was faxed to her by a friend. The magazine, which was located over two hours away (and in another state), was looking for a full-time (freelance) editor. Her pitch resulted in an interview at which she persuaded the managing editor to hire her, allow her to telecommute, and to be on site for only one week each month, when the resulting book was being put together for press.

Natural Remedies was a spin-off of *Vegetarian Times*. Meredith says, "The assignment was fabulous while it lasted. The publisher folded it after several issues, but because I had made contacts at *Vegetarian Times*, I was able to write back page essays for $750 on a fairly regular basis. Plus, this freelance editing assignment led to more substantial work (and pay) within the personal growth and holistic health industry. Not bad for one pitch letter, eh?"

While some might consider her statements in the pitch below blunt, I consider them a sign of self-confidence, industry tenure, and the obvious fact that she doesn't need to plead for a job by proving herself. The facts are obvious and her résumé proves she is qualified for the job.

Note: When a publisher is looking for a "full-time" freelance employee, you should negotiate for a telecommuting option! Most people who are required to work in-house, and on a full-time or almost full-time schedule under the direction of the employer, are employees, and deserve all the benefits associated with being an "employee" (insurance, payroll tax contributions, etc.). If you're a freelancer who is seeking a telecommuting position, please don't be fooled by firms that want to hire an in-house worker, but hope to avoid employment taxes and medical and other benefits simply by calling someone a "freelancer." For more on this topic, please see *"Your Rights As a Freelancer"* in this book.

If Meredith had not requested a telecommuting option, she'd have had to commute two hours each way to work...or look for other assignments. Remember, it never hurts to ask!

What makes Meredith's pitch a hit:
1. Direct, no-nonsense attitude.
2. Mentions reasons editors and writers alike enjoy working with her.
3. Mentions personal experience with alternative medicine.
4. Provides ample background information and materials.
5. Subtly requests in-person interview ("I'm curious to know whether the match is as good in person...") where she can wow them and then request a telecommuting option.

Meredith's tenure as a freelance editor for *Natural Remedies* lasted for three months before the publication folded. She earned $11,300.

Meredith's $11,300 Pitch

Date

Dear Mr. [Editor's Last Name],

You're looking for a freelance editor? I'm looking for a steady (and hefty) freelance assignment.

I've written about alternative medicine and holistic approaches since 1990. Two years ago, I bailed out a regional magazine Holistic Living, by serving as its interim editor for five issues.

Editors tend to like me because I beat deadlines, take editorial direction, and submit clean copy. Writers like being edited by me because I strive to bring out the best in their work without getting nasty.

A personal beneficiary of alternative medicine, I like taking part in educating a broader audience about it without being preachy, trendy, or dense.

Enclosed is almost too much material—my résumé, a partial list of publications, and a slew of clips.

My skills and experience seem to match your needs. I'm curious to know whether the match is as good in person as it appears to be on paper. I look forward to talking with you more about this opportunity at Natural Remedies.

Sincerely,

Meredith Gould

National Lawyers' Magazine - $6,000

Nader Anise is considered by many to be the nation's leading authority on lawyer marketing. His marketing expertise has been showcased, nationally, on NBC, PBS, Access Hollywood, Lawyers Weekly USA, Legal Management, and ABA Law Practice Management. He has lectured to ABA section attorneys and been featured in just about every major legal and marketing publication. Over the years, Nader has advised thousands of attorneys on the art of marketing. He has received national recognition for masterminding a public relations campaign that resulted in primetime television coverage and over $1 million in free publicity, while only costing $325 to implement. Nader is also an accomplished attorney, marketing professor, and author. The CLE Review of the American Law Institute-American Bar Association attests, "Nader Anise, Esq. is a nationally renowned lawyer marketing expert…" Nader can be reached via email at: nader@naderanise.com

~~~~~

Nader Anise's pitch was sent in response to an ad placed online seeking a regular contributor for *National Lawyers' Magazine*. In only four short paragraphs, Nader successfully proves that he's the perfect professional for the job.

I particularly like this statement: "My writing style adapts quite easily to any editorial style." Nader is obviously enthusiastic, flexible, and has the credentials required to write for an audience of attorneys.

In his pitch, Nader quotes the advertisement he saw, showing the editor that he actually read the ad. Many writers don't and often submit inappropriate queries. Editors recognize if a writer had read their ad or simply fired off a pitch to the most convenient email address!

What makes Nader's pitch a hit:
1. Enthusiastic, yet modest.
2. Nice formatting.
3. Quotes the job advertisement.
4. Offers complete bio and clips, but also an abbreviated bio in the body of the pitch (helpful for the busy editor!).

This pitch was sent via fax and resulted in 6 articles worth $1,000 each.

Nader's $6,000 Pitch

Date

Ms. [Editor's Full Name]
National Lawyers' Magazine
Mailing Address
City, State, Zip
SENT VIA FAX: (xxx)xxx-xxxx

RE: FREELANCE WRITING

Dear Ms. [Editor's Last Name],

I saw your listing in mediabistro.com and was thrilled because I have looked for a writing position such as this for a very long time. I believe I am a perfect match!

I have attached my profile and several clippings for your consideration. I think they demonstrate that "creative intellectualism" you are looking for. My writing style adapts quite easily to any editorial style. Moreover, my copy is clean--at least that's what many editors have said--and I do whatever it takes to meet my deadline: I have not missed one yet. Attention to detail is another one of my strong points and I'm easy to work with.

Please take a look at my qualifications and clips. I don't think you'll find a better-suited person for this position. *In case you want the 30-second bio summary, here it is:* I'm the founder of a successful law firm in South Florida--I started it over five years ago. I am also an MBA professor, professional legal speaker (member NSA) and nationally recognized lawyer marketing expert. In addition, I have written dozens of articles on law-related topics, have been featured on television numerous times, and founded the national legal association, ALPIA; American Lawyers Public Image Association. (See us at alpia.org). In short, I am the lawyer/writer/creative mind you have been looking for.

I would like to discuss freelancing for you in the immediate future. Please contact me at (xxx)xxx-xxxx to go over the details. Thank you in advance.

Very truly yours,

Nader Anise

Life Extension magazine - $6,480+

Dale Kiefer is a seasoned professional writer with extensive credits in a wide variety of print and electronic media. He is a former reporter for the Pittsburgh Post-Gazette and is co-author of The Buzz On Xtreme Sports. He is a former managing and contributing editor for Suite101.com, where he wrote and maintained the "Expectant Fathers" site for several years. Dale writes extensively on parenting issues: He has ghostwritten a book for the non-profit fatherhood skills-training organization, Boot Camp for New Dads, and continues to contribute to TheBabyCorner.com. Dale has a bachelor's degree in biological sciences and is a former Director of Continuing Medical Education for the laboratories at a large university medical center. He specializes in health, medical, and general science topics. Travel, art, and individual/extreme sports are his other areas of expertise. Dale lives with his family in Indianapolis where he pursues his passion for in-line skating, singing, and coaching his sons' soccer teams.

~~~~~

Dale Kiefer landed his first assignment from *Life Extension magazine* after responding to a classified advertisement gleaned from a writers' job board. *Life Extension magazine* is a nationally distributed, full-color print magazine covering new health and medical information from around the globe. Its editorial requirements include fairly technical, but layman-oriented, medical articles ranging from 2,500 – 3,500 words in length. Payment is $0.75 per word.

Several weeks after sending his pitch to *Life Extension magazine*, Dale essentially forgot all about this particular pitch. So, he was pleasantly surprised when the publication's editor-in-chief contacted him several months later.

In the first paragraph of his pitch below, Dale mentions his degree in biology, which is impressive and gives him an obvious edge when approaching publications seeking medical writers. Also, be sure to read his reference to interviewing medical professionals in his final paragraph. This short, succinct pitch letter makes it obvious Dale can handle medical writing assignments with ease.

After reading the pitch, the editor requested more material, including Dale's résumé and additional clips, which further demonstrated his ability to handle the kind of assignments they had in mind. After supplying relevant medical and technical clips and his résumé, and restating his "fervent desire to tackle the project(s)", Dale received his first assignment.

Dale adds, "Based on the editor-in-chief's assessment of my qualifications, he assigned me an important cover story, which was published promptly after submission. Payment was also prompt, and working with *Life Extension magazine* has been a pleasure. Since then, I have worked for this magazine continually to supply feature articles on any number of topics, mostly by assignment, although they are open to article suggestions."

What makes Dale's pitch a hit:
1. Mentions impressive qualifications in first paragraph.
2. Says he wants to offer "compelling features".
3. Very professional.
4. Mentions he's comfortable interviewing medical professionals and using their "lingo".
5. Leaves the possibility for assignments completely open, simply stating he looks forward to hearing from the editor.

Dale's first assignment from *Life Extension magazine* brought in $1,961.25. He said, "I could have earned more, but didn't feel comfortable jacking up the word count to the maximum allowed by

134

my contract; I felt I said what needed to be said without getting unnecessarily verbose."

Subsequent pieces have earned Dale $2,593.50 and $1928.25. He expects that his fourth and fifth articles for this client will earn about $2,500 each. This pitch was sent via email.

Dale's $6,480+ Pitch

Date

Dear [Editor's Name],

I'm very interested in writing compelling features for your nutrition magazine. I'm a professional writer with more than seven years experience writing for a wide variety of mainstream print and electronic publications. Although I've been a reporter for respected organizations such as the Pittsburgh Post-Gazette, and I have a minor in journalism, my degree is in biology.

I'm also a former Director of Continuing Medical Education for the clinical laboratories at a large university medical center. I'm well versed in analyzing complex clinical papers and extracting salient information for simplified (but never simplistic) presentation to a general audience. I've written everything from copy for full-scale advertising campaigns -- targeted at national and international audiences -- to consumer-oriented health articles.

I'm co-author of the book, "The Buzz On Xtreme Sports" - Lebhar Freidman Publishers, and I have ghostwritten a book, "Lessons from the Front Lines - Boot Camp for New Dads", which is pending publication.

Following, you will find a brief sample of some relevant work I have previously published. I'd like to emphasize that I am entirely comfortable interviewing medical professionals and speaking their lingo. I recognize the difference between scientific and pseudo-scientific claims and know how to critically and objectively evaluate -- and report on -- scientific data. I very much look forward to hearing from you.

Sincerely, Dale Kiefer

Expert Advice

Query Calls: How to Query by Phone
by Christine Greeley

For a writer, the query letter is the natural tool for securing work. Your query letter communicates your assets to the publishing world, and serves as an illustration of your writing talent.

But as your myriad queries are printed, stamped and mailed in all seriousness to the "Keepers of the Jobs," you may feel that sinking feeling in your writer's gut as you snap the mailbox closed and put up the flag (or click the "send button" in your email program).

"I may never hear from that editor. How will I know if they want me or not, when they requested in the ad that I don't call and bug them?" Then you wait. And wait. And wait. You sit at your desk and stare at the phone, your fingers itching to dial that editor's number. You stride to the mailbox, hopeful, then sweep out cobwebs, some of those nasty earwig bugs, and the utilities bill.

Let's roll back a minute. What about that telephone? It is true that most editors, publishers and agents are too overwhelmed with submissions to entertain new or follow-up queries by phone. However, there are many small publications, non-profit organizations and even large corporations that need help with writing, and *they* just don't know how to find it.

Now, I am not suggesting that you quit writing query letters and start "dialing for dollars." But how about translating the traditional query into a telephone call for some jobs?

Don't quit the day job just yet
In the beginning, my parents owned a business, and I began to view that as the backbone of my professional knowledge. I worked at my family's flower shop to pay the bills while trying to build my

freelance experience. I gained more professional expertise at a local Department of Defense contractor, while always on the lookout for a position in publishing. When I was hired at a nearby branch of a large publishing house that produced business newsletters, I was able to hone my editorial and writing skills with some solid knowledge of business writing behind me.

Eventually, I broke free. A colleague who left the company went to work for a non-profit organization. She hired me and another colleague to help her write journal reports. This gave me the confidence to leave the corporate safety net. I started working part-time again at the flower shop (for supplementary income), and dove into freelancing.

Find a connection!
One day at the shop, I picked up an industry newsletter published by a contractor for one of the major industry corporations. I truly admired the publication for its usefulness and great writing. Then it clicked: With more than ten years in the business, and being a writer as well, I would be the perfect freelance writer for this publication.

I picked up the phone, dialed the number and asked for the publisher by name. The conversation went something like this:

"Hi, I am a florist and also a freelance writer. I read your publication every month, and find it to be the most useful and well-written of all of them. Do you ever use freelance writers?"

"No. Tried that once. It's too much trouble."

I explained that when I worked as an editor, I found that using freelance writers was valuable because the company didn't have to pay them benefits, they worked on an as-needed basis, and many of them had expertise and contacts in the field they were covering.

"How about if I write something for you and you decide if I would be of help or not?"

"Okay, pitch me some ideas..."

And so I did. I suggested topics that I, as a florist, would have liked to see covered. He chose one, and liked what I submitted. Now, several years later, this client is my main income. In addition to writing features and interview-based profiles, and ghost writing for the resident industry expert, I have been called upon to perform editorial duties for him, proofreading and even helping with other projects outside of the publication. I have also taken this approach to secure regular writing work with a consumer-level veterinary care newsletter.

Major magazines are only a tiny portion of your market!
The point is, just because you are a writer, and you desire fame and fortune as the fruit of your talent, it doesn't mean you have to hop on the traditional publishing treadmill of magazines and books to find your niche. Explore what you know and then look for an outlet for writing on the subject. Did you have a job in the past where you gained a great deal of knowledge about that industry or your job there? Do you have a passion or hobby? Or is there something that you would like to learn in-depth so you can write about it professionally? Even being a parent has given you experiences that you could apply to consumer markets, such as product descriptions in toy catalogs or parenting newsletters.

Here are some alternative types of publications and firms to investigate and pitch your ideas to:

> **Industry Newsletters**. Just like my florist business newsletter, there are trade newsletters for dentists, nurses, pharmaceuticals, hardware stores, and agriculture, just to name a few. If you have knowledge

to offer to a specific industry, search for newsletters that serve that industry online, or visit the office of a local business, ask if they subscribe to any industry newsletters, and then ask if you can have a copy They'll probably be very happy to share. Then study the newsletter, noting the style, topics and, of course the editor's name and contact information.

> **Corporate Newsletters**. These are usually produced in-house and are used to communicate company information to employees, other divisions, and even contractors. Pitch some ideas and try to get your foot in the door. This type of work may lead to other jobs such as production of their newsletter, press releases or journal reporting.

> **Small Business Customer Newsletters**. The local garden center, wine shop, or bookstore may put out a newsletter for their customer base, covering topics of interest in the business's niche. While these publications often contain intriguing editorial content (to keep the customer interested), they are primarily a marketing vehicle for the business. If you know of or frequent a business that doesn't yet produce a customer newsletter, contact the owner and offer to write and publish their first and subsequent issues.

> **Municipal Communications**. Your local library, town hall, government organizations, and agencies such as the senior citizen or youth halls may publish fliers and brochures explaining their services. They may also put out annual reports or submit information for a town-wide annual report. This is not glamorous work, but it could bring in some cash as well as make many contacts for you. Research each one to find a contact name and either phone them to offer your services, or

send a professional proposal by mail or email. Be sure to emphasize your status as a local citizen.

> **Non-profit organizations**. Many non-profits publish annual reports, journals, and solicitation materials. For some, hiring a freelancer to write for them is more economical than having someone on staff that they have to pay on a regular basis.

Pitch yourself

Like query letters, phone queries have their own set of guidelines. Before picking up that phone, write a phone script for yourself. This will help you sound professional and articulate. Be sure to practice it a few times to make sure you don't sound like you are reading a script.

A good query call should include an appropriate salutation, introduction, positive comment on the contact's business, your proposal, an offer to make an appointment (if necessary) or to send samples and a written proposal, a request to make a follow up call, thank you, and goodbye.

Sample Phone Query

Here is a sample for phone query used to pitch the creation and publication of a new newsletter. If a company already has a newsletter, you can adapt this script accordingly.

Good morning, Ms. Duffy. My name is Julie Smith, and I visit Duffy's Fine Wine whenever I plan to entertain guests. I am impressed with the array of wines you carry as well as the nice selection of accessories.

Your customer service has always been great, too, since you are able to make excellent suggestions that never fail to please my guests. I am not just a wine aficionado, though, I'm also a writer. I've been thinking about how useful a monthly newsletter could be to your customers. You could advertise your wine tastings and other events, while profiling new arrivals and old favorites and other items of interest.

I would like to discuss with you how I could help you get your monthly newsletter written professionally without your having to spend valuable time doing it. And, offering a regular newsletter will entice your customers to return on a more frequent basis! I realize you are probably busy right now, so could we schedule an appointment to talk?

I am looking forward to meeting with you. Thanks for your time... Have a great day. Goodbye.

Of course, any phone script you develop could also be easily used as a written query. But when you are pursuing work with a small business or publisher, it may be more effective to first try to make person-to-person contact. In a two-way discussion, you'll be able to sell your knowledge in concert with your writing experience, answer questions, and determine the prospective client's exact needs. It's a different avenue for your job hunt, a non-traditional way to get more writing work!

Christine Greeley is a freelance writer and editor living in Connecticut. While she writes primarily for niche industry newsletters in floristry and veterinary care, she has also edited and written brochures for municipalities, medical journal entries, and business training materials. When inspired appropriately, she will put away the word processor and take out the drawing implements to dabble in illustration and graphic design. Christine can be reached by email at drewdots@aol.com.

Six Golden Rules of Queries and Submissions... and How I Broke Them!
By Bob Freiday

Hi. I'm Bob, a freelance writer with over a decade of experience and 700+ articles, stories and book chapters under my belt. I've written for over 50 publications in those twelve years - and I have some advice on "the rules" of freelance writing, and how I broke most of them in order to succeed in the freelance writing industry. I hope you enjoy this piece, which Angela invited me to write for this book.

Rule #1: Expect 12 rejections for each acceptance

Yeah, right! Granted, I did get a slew of rejections (about six in a row) when I first started sending out unsolicited stories for the adult "men's market." (Hey-- don't judge *me!* It was *my wife's* idea!!) Yeah, that was my approach when I first decided to get paid for my words...sending out stories I'd already written. I soon learned that writers simply do not have to live by this Golden Rule. Twelve rejections for each acceptance? What business could possibly survive with that average? Why should a writing business accept it? As I've told many fledgling freelancers - operating as a full-time freelance writer is not *like* running a business, it *is* running a business.

Simply put, you should always sell everything you write. How? By simply *selling it* before you write it!

As Angela's explaining with this book-- *get the sale* by querying the editor, *then* write it. That mean's the story you're now writing is *already sold!* If you do it that way, you will basically be selling *everything you write!* The only catch to that, of course, is that you must *deliver* what you promise (i.e., get the assignment first, deliver the goods as promised, and you *will*, I promise, sell everything you write).

Back when I was stupidly sending out unsolicited stories to the adult men's market, I suddenly realized that I was rushing too much; that I wasn't studying the markets closely enough. I slowed down,

> Operating as a full-time freelance writer is not *like* running a business, it *is* running a business.

read 12 copies of a particular publication (Chic Letters), then sent out a small story. A few weeks later I received a brief, non-personal, form-letter type response--with a check for $15. Wow! I was published! In Chic Letters!

And that's when I immediately broke another "Golden Rule" about querying:

Rule #2: Never, EVER telephone a busy editor
Uh, huh. Sure. When I got that $15 check in New Jersey, I immediately grabbed the phone and called Hollywood, California to speak to the editor who'd bought my story. The guy who got on the phone was rather gruff, and obviously very busy. "YEAH!!?"

And I was, like, "Well... uhmmm... you just bought one of my stories, Sir, and I was wondering if I might sell more to you. Is there a way to send you more than one at a time? What's the normal process with writers?"

And he was, like, "What!? Who the (bleep!) are *you?* I deal with hundreds of writers. What did you write?"

I told him the name of my little story, and he goes, "Oh! That one! That was great! Send me packages of twelve at a time, whatever categories you want -- but try to mix them up a little bit. I'll buy what I want, and send you a check for whatever ones I buy. Send me 12 at a time -- okay? I gotta' go. Bye!"

Now, if I'd never made that phone call, I'd never have known to send "packages" instead of single stories. My next package was

12 little stories, and he bought all 12. Instead of a $15 check in the mail, I got one for $180. My wife and I couldn't believe it! I sent out another 12, of course, and the editor kept buying and buying and buying -- an Energizer Bunny® editor hungry for Quality Trash!

A non-rule, but a great tip for all writers: Don't be afraid to ask for favors – and *network!!*
After a few rounds of that, I broke the rules again and, one more time, dialed Hollywood.

"WHAAAT!!??" the unpleasant man answered.

I explained who I was again, and he was a little more friendly, realizing he was on a gravy train with me. He'd bought close to fifty little stories from me in barely two months. As delicately as possible, I explained that I was the father of four kids and hoping he might be able to point me to an editor who bought "larger pieces for higher pay," with, of course, a promise not to stop sending *him* material, as well.

He immediately gave me the name of an editor at a much larger publishing company in the men's adult market, and said to me, "Tell her I sent you. She pays, like, one-fifty or two-hundred a story, I think."

I quickly telephoned the editor (no names, please), and she proceeded to tell me that she was "real busy" but definitely looking for writers. "Call me at home tonight," she said, surprising me. "Here's my number." I called her at home that night. We spoke for well over an hour, and she gave me two immediate assignments worth $200 apiece. BINGO! Four-hundred bucks in business -- 'cause I'd broken the rules *twice* and telephoned *two* editors, rather than contacting them via query letter.

Soon after I began writing regularly for the editor who paid $200 a pop, I was perusing PC Magazine and read in John Dvorak's column a fascinating little story about something that very few people had ever heard of: Computer Viruses. What? Interesting. Intriguing, I thought. (Remember, this was a long time ago.) I read the story, realized that *this* could *definitely* be something *any* editor at *any* business magazine might be interested in hearing about, so I grabbed my Writer's Market and began flipping through the pages trying to find a reasonably mid-range publication that just might take a shot with a writer who'd never published anything "major" for a mainstream publisher. I didn't want to mention my erotic writing, so knew I had little to tout regarding writing experience.

Anyway, I decided to break the rules again. But, this time, I decided I wanted to break *two* rules. Of course, I was now used to breaking the "don't telephone busy editors" rule, but now I wanted to do something I'd always read in Writers Digest and elsewhere that writer's simply shouldn't do:

Rule #3: Never write an article "on spec" (on speculation); always get a contract
My thinking was this: It was highly unlikely that I'd ever *get* the assignment with little or no experience writing about business and management, nor about computers or software. I was fighting an uphill battle, but suspected I had "the key" to getting my first honest-to-gosh "mainstream" assignment with a nationally-distributed business publication.

I was hungry, in a hurry, and enthused about this idea. To this day, about 16 years later, I can still remember the conversation:

"Hello. Sorry to bother you, but I promise to be quick. I'm a freelance writer in New Jersey, and I just found out about a shocking situation in the computer world that I thought you and your readers might be interested in, and was hoping I could run it by you real quick?"

I had the editor's interest immediately. "Sure. What's up?"

I explained about the story I'd just read, and how this "virus" had infected the computers at Lehigh University's computer lab in Pennsylvania, that it had completely erased all of their hard-drive materials, and that many experts believed that it was possibly the most dangerous thing facing business today, and that all managers and supervisors who used computers needed to know about it. (Her publication was a Simon & Schuster/Prentice-Hall newsletter called "Supervisor's Bulletin.") I then explained to her that I was just an "up and coming" writer, but that I had full confidence I could write a good story for her. I also added that I'd be more than willing to "write the piece on spec," meaning that there would be no hard feelings if she didn't buy it. "I just don't want to pursue the story with your publication in mind unless I know that you'll definitely buy it if it's up to your standards."

She agreed immediately. "That sounds fair. I like that idea. No hard feelings if I don't buy it, though, right?"

We both agreed. She told me that, if she bought it, she'd pay $0.10 per word, which she paid all of her "new writers." The story would be targeted at between 1,500 and 2,000 words. I sent a story that turned out to be 1,875 words, so my first "real" paycheck from a "real," honest-to-gosh, serious publishing company was for $187.50. And, once again, I'd done it by (oops!!) *breaking the rules!!*

Then, of course, I called back and "networked," and she gave me the names of *four other editors* who she thought would be interested in working with me. She also gave me another assignment over the phone to boot! And that, ladies and gentleman, was the catalyst that truly launched my career. I could barely keep up with the work, after that, parlaying one sale to one editor into a new assignment with a new editor, and on and on and on, 'till I found myself writing for *over a dozen editors in two buildings!*

All because I broke the rules.

Rule #4: Write about what you know
Yeah, sure! I'm gonna write about running a high-speed slitter in a plastics factory? I'm gonna write about running a gigantic vacuum metallizer at another plastics factory? I'm gonna write about blowing up three cars in two years while running around the state as a rock-n-roll advertising salesman? I'm gonna write about baking bagels in a small bakery?

I'll tell you this much...I sure didn't know much about Credit & Collections before writing over 60 articles about that. I sure didn't know much about Corporate and Industrial Security before writing probably 100 stories about *that.* I sure didn't know much about Warehousing, Logistics, Computer Integrated Manufacturing (CIM), Robotics, Just-In-Time (JIT) Distribution and things of that nature before publishing another hundred stories about *those* fascinating topics.

I mean, really! What kind of stupid rule *is* that? "Write About What You Know." Give me a break! You write about what you want to learn about! I'd often read something fascinating in the paper, or see it on CNN or somewhere else on television, or read about it in a trade publication, and then pitch an article about it so I could interview the experts, learn about the topic more deeply, and then write a fascinating article.

That's what *real* writers do. They don't write about picking daisies in their back yard or weeding their gardens. Really! They write about fascinating topics they want to learn about, and usually with the assignment already in the bag.

Which leads me to yet another Golden Rule:

Rule #5: Write the best article you can, then send it to your target markets

As with many beginning writers, this "rule" was somehow drilled into me from a young age. You write an interesting piece, polish it, then methodically keep sending it out as it bounces back until, somehow and miraculously, somebody expresses an interest, and it *sticks!!* You make a sale!!

Truth be told, and as touched upon earlier, few writers sell material in this way. In my earlier example of writing on speculation, I didn't secure a contract from that editor before doing the work, but I did secure her interest and her intent to buy if the article met her expectations. So, it was not a blind submission.

Of course, there actually are editors (many in the fiction genre, many in the adult market) who *ask* their regular writers to write the material and send it, assuming the writer knows the magazine well enough to write a good piece, but that's different. You're being personally invited by the editor to send in the un-assigned story, so it really isn't "unsolicited" anymore.

Generally speaking, though, ignore the above rule. Come up with a great idea, target the market (in whichever order), do the research, write a great query that really teases the editor (makes him/her want to read more!), and then send it out. Although I broke all the rules and used the telephone, what I did was basically the same thing: I'd target a market, come up with an article idea, do the research, design my "tease," and query the editor.

That is the method by which I sold 99% of my 700+ articles. Surely *you* can use it to sell your first hundred--eh?

And, finally:

Rule #6: Start with smaller markets and work your way up
As stated above, my first sale was to Chic Letters, a widely-circulated, nationally-distributed men's magazine. My next forty-eight sales were to the same company, but some also appeared in Hustler Fantasies and two other major erotica publications where the stories were freely distributed by the buyer. (He had a contract to provide content for all four publications.) And, my next hundred or so stories were to other "major" men's markets.

Start small? *Why?*

But, with no "real" non-fiction writing credits to my name, my first "mainstream" sale (the computer-virus story I told you about earlier) was to *the largest publishing company in the world!* Simon & Schuster/Prentice-Hall, at that time, was the world's largest publishing company, but I didn't let that intimidate me! (You shouldn't let the size of the publication or publishing company intimidate you, either.)

The bottom line? Can you write well enough to crack that market? Only you know the answer to that. Don't be afraid to submit intelligent, well-written query letters to "major" markets, even if you're "new" to the business.

Rule #7: Always read at least several copies of a particular publication you plan to query
This is another Golden Rule I constantly find myself breaking! While you should study the publication to learn their style, their tone, and their editorial attitude, several issues is a bit extreme. You can often find samples of their editorial content on their website. "You really must know a publication in order to effectively write for them." Unless, of course, you're a rebel like me.

Don't miss Bob Freiday's new book, 10 Golden Rules of Freelance Writing and How I Broke Them (How to Break the Rules and Make It As a Magazine Writer)! It's available as a paperback and an instantly downloadable ebook at: http://www.writersweekly.com/books/1368.html

Want to get more freelance writing assignments? Want to increase your writing income? Are you willing to break some rules to get what you want? Then this book is for you! Bob Freiday is a disobedient writer, chronically breaking the Top 10 Golden Rules of Freelance Writing, and subsequently landing those elusive, high-paying assignments that other writers covet! You can learn more about Bob online at http://www.scribeguy.com or send an email to ScribeGuy@ScribeGuy.com.

Your Rights as a "Freelancer"
by Angela Hoy

As an advocate for writers' rights, over the past few years I have discovered that many in-house "freelancers" are the victims of ongoing illegal employment practices.

Beware of firms that advertise for freelancers but require those "freelancers" to work in-house. An increasing problem in many industries is to advertise for "freelance" workers, but require them to work in-house. Many firms hope that, by calling their employees "freelancers", they can avoid paying employment (payroll) taxes, overtime and other benefits (medical insurance, disability, worker's compensation if you're injured, and even unemployment insurance and benefits). Some business owners, whether through ignorance or malicious intent, think that a simple title change can eliminate their liability in these employment law areas. Once the government catches up with them, they find out how wrong they are!

Federal employment laws are firm in this area. If you're working at their location, using their tools, and operating under their primary direction, you are probably an employee and eligible for benefits. How I analyze this scenario in my mind is to think about myself hiring a plumber. He comes to my house and works in my house (in-house), but he uses his own tools, sets his own hours, and works under his own direction. (I, of course, know nothing about plumbing, so I can't supervise him.) If something I have needs to be repaired and is portable, he can take it home with him and fix it at his location and under his own terms. In fact, other than the fact that I ordered his services and will pay him upon completion, I have no control or input regarding his job whatsoever. He's a professional, gave me a quote, did the work, my toilet was repaired, and I paid him. This plumber is a contractor (freelancer).

But, if I owned a large building with 100 toilets, I would need a full-time plumber – someone available to work for me during all or most business hours, under my direction, and under my terms. He'd use my tools (not many plumbers have enough equipment to service 100 toilets). Since he's working primarily for me (he may have other private clients that he services after-hours, but that's irrelevant), under my direction, using my tools, and at my location, he's an employee. (Hey, even if you're using your own computer (equipment) but still meet the other criteria above, you're probably still an employee.)

Even part-time employees are eligible for some benefits. If you're self-employed, you have to pay both portions of your FICA and Medicare taxes. If you're an employee (even a part-timer), the employer must pay half of that expense. This amount can be quite significant, and your employer knows this! In addition, many employers claim their employees are not eligible for overtime based on their position or title. (Basically, if your position is not supervisory and you're working in-house and under the direction of another, you are probably eligible for overtime. To read the precise criteria for this, see the link below. Even some supervisors are eligible for overtime.)

So, what in the world does this have to do with queries and this book? Well, you may find some very appealing jobs listed online and in newspapers soliciting in-house freelancers. And, knowing what you now know, you may be able to convince those "employers" to allow you to telecommute.

Never hesitate to ask an employer who is hiring for an in-house freelance position if you can telecommute. First, explain to them the difference between a freelancer and an employee. Be kind and friendly so they won't feel you're investigating them or being accusatory. They may simply be ignorant of the law.

Explain to the prospective employer the benefits of hiring a freelancer (no employment taxes, no medical, disability, worker's compensation or unemployment insurance, no equipment expenses or office space, no office supplies, no vacation or sick pay, and no overtime.). And then offer to work for them as a telecommuting freelancer for an hourly rate (be prepared to quote a rate!).

How much should you charge? I am asked this question often and there is no standard fee. But, I strongly encourage you to charge an hourly rate rather than a flat fee. Project scopes can change daily and trying to squeeze more money out of a firm later, even when the changes are their fault, is difficult, if not impossible. Basically, you should determine how much money you want to make per hour, add a bit to that (many people underestimate their worth!) and quote that rate. If they balk at the figure, either offer to negotiate a lower rate now with a higher rate kicking in three months later, or simply walk away. Never agree to work for less than your desired rate because you will never be happy with your pay, you will feel undervalued, and your self-esteem will take a beating. And, despite the fact that most people think they can write (meaning they think it's an easy job and that writers don't deserve respectable pay rates), the fact is that the general population CAN'T write well and you have a valuable talent that is sought after in most industries. Always remember that!

If the prospective employer/client continues to insist you work in-house but as a "freelancer" (no benefits), let them know that you know the difference between an employee and a contractor (in case they're trying to hire an employee without paying taxes and benefits). While this may mean an abrupt end to your meeting (or email/phone discussion), this may convince them to allow you to telecommute (if they're simply ignorant of the law). If they still insist you work in-house but with no benefits (or tell you to get lost), you should immediately report them to the Department of Labor. Contact the office below and tell them an employer tried to hire you for an in-house job requiring xx hours per week of work, but offered you no benefits, including payroll taxes.

The Department of Labor has an information page that describes employee types and their overtime eligibility:
http://www.dol.gov/esa/regs/compliance/whd/whdfs17.htm

Complaints should be reported to the Department of Labor's Wage and Hour Division by calling: 1-866-4USWAGE (1-866-487-9243)

Or, find your local office at:
http://www.dol.gov/esa/contacts/whd/america2.htm

So, is that prospective employer/client hiring a contractor (freelancer!) or an employee? The College of Charleston has published a very handy chart where individuals can determine if they are, indeed, contractors or employees in the eyes of the IRS.

Internal Revenue Service 20 Rule Test for Establishing Employment Relationship – Employer-Employee vs. Independent Contractor can be found online at:
http://www.orga.cofc.edu/resources_irs20rule.html

The pdf version is here:
http://www.orga.cofc.edu/resources_irs20rule.pdf

You can review the Fair Labor Standards Act online at:
http://www.dol.gov/esa/whd/flsa

Angela Hoy's Secret for Finding Steady Freelance Work

When I surf the Internet each week looking for freelance writing jobs to post in WritersWeekly.com, the job sites always return a large number of jobs that aren't really freelance writing jobs…but full-time, in-house editorial jobs. The reason these results come up when searching the job sites is because the editorial jobs usually include the term "freelance writer" in their job descriptions. Why? Well, on further investigation, I find these types of statements in their job descriptions:

Must hire and work with freelance writers…

Must have existing relationship with freelance writers…

Must edit articles by freelance writers…

But, wait… Some of these firms are large, well-known firms…firms I have never found running ads seeking freelancers. Who are those writers who are working for these firms and how did they land those gigs? Quite simply, they're the ones who have gotten their foot in the proverbial door in creative ways.

Many large firms know that running ads for freelance writers may bring a deluge of résumés that they don't have time to sift through. Since these firms don't run ads for freelancers, this means that, when you do approach them for work, you have a much better chance of having your résumé read and of being hired to do occasional or ongoing freelance writing for them. And, creativity in approaching them is the key!

One way for you to find firms that are secretly using freelance writers is to search the large job sites. For example, surf on over to http://www.monster.com, and click that "search jobs" box up there on the left. Now, type "freelance writers" (yes, include the quotes and make sure it's writers in the plural form, not writer) in that top box. Click "Select All" under the two boxes that follow (choose location and choose job category). Now, click the "Sort Results by: Date" button down there at the bottom and then click "Get Results."

Okay, as of this writing, the most recent job I can find is for a website that is hiring a full-time, in-house managing editor. Nowhere online can I find that they're hiring freelance writers, or that they've ever run ads seeking freelancers. But, in the managing editor's job description, it states, "must have experience in cultivating and working with freelance writers."

Voila! This firm doesn't runs ads for freelance writers, yet they're using them! So, how do you approach this firm? Quite simply, you should create a form pitch letter like the Abbi Perrets form letter (which appears in an earlier chapter) and send it to the "Managing Editor" at this firm (or whatever title is listed in the ad). While you don't know them by name, you may mention that you know they're new (that you saw an ad for their position on monster.com) and that you'd be honored to be one of their freelance writers.

Let's find some more job listings and see how they reveal they are using freelance writers on a regular basis.

Again, using monster.com and searching for the term "freelance writers", I found ads for the following positions that hire or supervise freelancers for each respective firm. Once you click on the ad, use the search function in your browser to find the word "freelance" in the ad itself (so you don't have to read the entire ad. Some firms are pretty long-winded.):

Copywriter / Editor
"Manage vendor relationships including identifying, interviewing, and assessing the quality of new freelance writers..."
-Catholic Relief Services

Editorial Manager/Team Leader
"Leader will work closely with medical directors, contributing medical editors, and freelance writers."
-Baylor College of Medicine

Managing Editor
"Coordinates any use of freelance or other external copy resources."
-BestBuy.com

Communications Specialist
"Develop and manage a network of freelance writers."
Millennium Pharmaceuticals

Medical Writer
"Contract with freelance writers and coordinate schedule of deliverables and payment of invoices."
-Newton Gravity Shift

Senior Editor
"...work closely with freelance journalists and authors to develop articles of interest relating to corporate finance."
- The American Institute of CPA's

And those are just a few of the listings that popped up on only one job site! Try my method using these popular employment websites as well:

http://www.careerbuilder.com

http://www.creativehotlist.com

http://hotjobs.yahoo.com

http://www.jobbank.gc.ca

http://newslink.org/newjoblinksearch.html

http://www.nytimes.com/pages/jobs/index.html

http://www.careercast.com/js.php

http://www.wantedjobs.com/jsp/search.jsp?cb=wjo

http://www.employment911.com/jobs/job-search.aspx

Index

About the Author

In 1997, after finding no current source of paying markets for writers in print or online, Angela Hoy founded WritersWeekly.com. Angela subsequently became an activist for freelancers, fighting for the rights of writers and working to change industry standards that leave writers (starving artists) in dire financial straits while feeding the giant, profitable publishing conglomerates. She also created WritersWeekly Whispers and Warnings, a place where writers can warn their colleagues about unethical publishers and editors.

Angela and Richard Hoy run WritersWeekly.com and Booklocker.com from their home on the Penobscot River in Bangor, Maine. Angela and Richard believe that children are happiest with their parents, so all their "employees" also work from their own homes. Angela and Richard are the proud parents of Zach, Ali, Frank, and Max.

WritersWeekly.com, the largest-circulation freelance writing ezine in the world, is the FREE marketing emag for writers featuring new freelance job listings and paying markets every Wednesday. Subscribe today at: http://www.writersweekly.com

New subscribers receive the <u>free guide</u>, *How to Be a Freelance Writer* (includes 103 paying markets!).

Booklocker.com, your bookstore for the unique, eclectic, and different, publishes electronic and print on demand (POD) books for authors. **Your book can be published as a glossy paperback or hardcover in only 4 to 6 weeks and for as little as $217!** High royalties, monthly royalty payments, and authors keep all rights to their books. For details, see: http://www.booklocker.com/getpublished/published.html

Angela's Other Books:

· How to Be a Syndicated Newspaper Columnist (includes database of 6,000+ newspapers and 100+ syndicates)

· Profitable Email Publishing: How to Publish a Profitable Emag

· How to Write, Publish and Sell Ebooks

· How to Publish and Promote Online (co-written with M.J. Rose)

· The Emergency Divorce Handbook for Women (available in paperback; but **the ebook version is free as a public service to all women** at: http://www.angelahoy.com/book)

Angela's Publications:

· WritersWeekly.com – **FREE** via email every Wednesday

· The Write Markets Report - $11.95/year. See: http://www.writersweekly.com/index-twmr.htm

Angela's Fun 6-Week Online Class!

· How to Remember, Write and Publish Your Life Story For more details, see: http://www.angelahoy.com

Printed in the United States
55229LVS00002B/30